Yes

We Can Love One Another!

CATHOLICS and PROTESTANTS
CAN SHARE A COMMON FAITH

Revised Edition

Warren R. Angel

Warren R. Angel
P.O. Box 1133
Bonsall, CA 92003

Blog and website: **www.theangelreport.net**
E-mail: **warrenrangel@cox.net**

YES WE CAN LOVE ONE ANOTHER!
Catholics and Protestants *Can* Share a Common Faith

First Edition, 1997
Revised Edition, 2019

Printed in the United States of America

Unless otherwise noted, Scripture references are from the following sources:

Copyedited by Rose Hamill

ISBN 0-9654806-0-7
ISBN 978-0-9654806-0-4

Publisher's Cataloging in Publication (prepared by Quality Books Inc.)

Angel, Warren.
        Yes we can love one another!: Catholics and Protestants can share a common faith/by Warren Angel.
        p. cm.
        Includes bibliographical references.
        Preassigned LCCN: 96-94822
        ISBN 0-9654806-0-7
1. Catholic Church—Relations—Protestantism. 2. Protestantism—Relations—Catholic Church. 3. Church—Unity. 1. Title.
BV601.5.A64 1997   230
                                                                        QBI96-40533

To my mother, Madeline, and
and my father, Russell,
who loved the Church

Contents

Preface to the Revised Edition   1

Preface   5

1. The First Century Church as the Model for Our Common Faith   11

2. Anyone Can Understand the Church's Book of Faith and History   39

3. The Christ of the New Testament Is Our Source of Spiritual Power and Contentment   55

4. We Can Still Have the Faith of Mary and Paul   75

5. Fellowship Through Christ's Spiritual Calling   99

6. Because God Loves Us, We Can Love and Respect One Another   133

7. Sharing the Joy as Servants of Jesus Christ   157

Endnotes   185

Index   189

Preface to the Revised Edition

Much has changed in both the world and the Church since *Yes We Can Love One Another!* was first published in 1997. The world has become a more mean-spirited environment, especially in the political arena as people and nations vie for power. And the Church, for a variety of reasons, has split further apart in some areas as individuals also vie for power in the false notion that only their beliefs and practices are correct.

It was true in 1997 that not everything done in the name of Christ was the will of God, nor based on the truth of His Word. That is even more true today. The Bible's teachings and the beliefs of some who claim to be Christian are often widely divergent.

This is dramatically evident in the matter of sexual abuse in the Church. A number of years ago a ministry colleague told me the problem was prolific in the Catholic Church. I still don't think the problem was as common as he thought, but since many stories have recently come to light it is obvious that sexual abuse in the RCC has been more widespread than most people imagined. To their shame, through non-Christian, uncaring attitudes, more than a few bishops covered up much of this unchristian and even criminal activity by priests. A few Catholics have left the RCC because of these revelations, and some Protestants detest Catholicism more than ever.

Protestants, however, are merely hypocrites when pointing their fingers, writing angry diatribes against the Catholic Church, and telling Catholics that they must leave their church or face the wrath of an angry God. The truth is that Protestants have also been guilty of blatant sexual abuse, not just by infamous televangelists, but by pastors and ministers in virtually every denomination and in many non-denominational contemporary churches. The recent revelations in the Southern Baptist Convention of widespread sexual abuse, especially of ministers abusing women and girls, have shocked Christ-loving Christians who had no idea of the problem.

This problem among Protestants, however, is not confined to the SBC.

I personally know of more than a handful of Protestant ministers who have been guilty of sexual sins, some of whom have been ignored or excused by their fellow clergy.

Before God, however, the Church has no excuse for sexual or any other sins. Still, most Catholics I know and talk to have never seen or heard of any misconduct on the part of priests. I do not mean to belittle the abuse in the RCC, nor in the SBC. It is shamefully and blatantly *evil.* Those who have committed crimes should be in jail. They will answer to God for their sins.

However, that being said and that being true, it is also true that most priests and ministers are wonderful, holy servants of Jesus Christ. Catholics are not going to leave their church because Christ is still their Savior, and the worldwide Church is still Christ's Church. Christ is righteous, loving, and true to God His Father.

And He is not responsible for the evils being uncovered and, in some places, still being committed.

Priests who have not Christ's spirit or power in their lives, nor concern for those who were entrusted to their care, are responsible for their own willful and unchristian actions. The same can be said for Protestant ministers who violate their trusts and act as though they have no faith and belief in Christ nor love for God and humanity.

Christians—both Protestants and Catholics—are called to holy living and to love one another as Jesus commanded (John 13:34-35). The command to love one another also calls us and empowers us to help and restore those fallen into sin. Leaving Christ's Church is not an option.

Another reason all of us, as believers in Christ, need to hang together as bands of brothers and sisters is because the threat of violent persecution hangs threateningly over our heads. More than 250 million Christians face persecution from Muslims, Communists, Buddhists, Hindus, and dictatorial regimes and factions as I write these words. At least 4000 believers in Christ have been killed in the past year. Some think the number is much higher inasmuch as statistics are hard to come by.

According to Open Doors' Watch List 2019 (see www.opendoorsusa.org), North Korea is the worst nation in the world for Christians. But, surprisingly, India has made the Top 10 because of Hindu violence against Christians. Muslims remain the worst offenders with 33 of the top 50 nations where Christians experience persecution.

Protestants and Catholics do come together, pray together, work together, and help protect one another when the violence of persecution is at their doorsteps, especially in places such as China, Colombia, and Muslim nations. They all come to love one another, appreciate one another, and help one another as brothers and sisters in Christ.

Yet Jesus Christ's prayer (John 17:20-23) that all of His followers would be one in love and power and purpose has still never been fully answered. But He believed not only that it *should* be but that it *could* be. My prayer is still that this small book will help Christians love one another and so answer Christ's prayer.

It is well *past time* that this should be so!

Warren R. Angel
June, 2019
California

Preface

Ever since several Catholic and Protestant leaders issued a declaration of Christian fellowship and mission in March of 1994 (*Evangelicals and Catholics Together: The Christian Mission in the Third Millennium*), a number of books have appeared warning against the evils of Catholicism. Paranoia runs rampant among some Protestants that any dialogue and association with Catholics will be the beginning of the end of the true Church and, eventually, as heresy, ignorance, and apathy lull us into a false sense of Christian brotherhood, the superchurch of the Antichrist will have engulfed us all.

There is some reality in the fears regarding an ecumenical superchurch, for institutional ecumenism seems willing to admit any group claiming to be Christian, whether it is a true follower of Christ or not. But what few evangelical Protestants are willing to admit or even recognize is that the false church is *already* in our midst and has been since the first century. Most of the New Testament, even the Gospels, was written to combat heresy both present and future, heresy which, whether ultra-dogmatic fundamentalism or faithless liberalism, has persistently denied, in one form or another, the divinity and efficacy of Jesus Christ, the Son of God who came and died for the sins of humanity.

We find this same kind of denial among both Catholics and Protestants today, sometimes in rather amazing places!

On the other hand, the Church endures in every nation of our world because men and women of varying cultures and traditions have steadfastly refused to believe falsehoods and have clung, even in a martyr's death both in the early days of the Church and in certain countries now, to the Christ who loves them.

Yet many Christians are slow to understand that people who really love Jesus, follow Him diligently, and share His love with others, are not uniquely found in any one of the vast array of Protestant denominations and sects, nor under the umbrella of a varied and worldwide Catholicism.

I know Catholics who love Jesus Christ just as much as any Protestant. Protestants who criticize efforts to promote fellowship with Catholics champion a doctrinal purity, which they believe is quite foreign to Catholics still locked into a medieval theology void of any understanding of justification by faith. (Many Catholics of Martin Luther's day *did* understand this concept. Some modern evangelical Protestants do *not.*)

Doctrinal purity, however, is never to be preferred over love for Christ, a fact He pointed out to the Church at Ephesus late in the first century (Revelation 2:4). This has often been forgotten or ignored by the Church of history. The modem Church is no exception. I believe we must strive for truth, but never at the expense of love for Jesus Christ and love for one another.

Furthermore, Protestants themselves have never been free from error. No sooner did the ink dry on Luther's *95 Theses* than the Reformers began battling back and forth mercilessly over theology and practice. Protestants have continued the sometimes acrimonious squabbles to the present day.

I hope it will come as a relief to those concerned with yet another Protestant minister urging fellowship and mission with all Christians, both Catholic and Protestant, that I have no interest in institutional ecumenism. Neither do I have an interest in getting believers to change churches. My only reason for writing this book is to nurture love and understanding—*on a personal level*—among all who truly love Jesus Christ and claim to be His disciples.

After all, if we really love Jesus Christ, why can't we love one another? He believed that we could. He prayed that we would. In John 10:16 Jesus said that His Church would be "one flock, one shepherd." And in John 17:20-21 the prayer of Jesus for His Church was in part that "all of them may be one, Father, just as you are in me and I am in you. May they also be in us so that the world may believe that you have sent me."

Yet despite Jesus' belief and prayer, the Church has never known the love and harmony which He believed it could achieve. I am not sure that it ever will be such a Church, but I do know that *it is past time for all Christians to come to the place of love and understanding and fellowship, and appreciation of and for every brother and sister in Christ.*

If we cannot do this we have no right to call ourselves Jesus' disciples—the very meaning of the word "Christian." We are merely religious devotees, unloving, and certainly unlike our Savior Jesus Christ who loved Jew and Samaritan and Gentile alike, and who sent His disciples not to those they knew and liked, but to *all* the people of the world.

Furthermore, the barbarians are knocking at the gate. The world is ripe for evangelism, but at the same time the forces of evil are gathering, stronger than ever, to rid the world of evil's number one pest—Christianity. The Church needs to stand as one—one in love, one in power in the Holy Spirit, and one in mission and purpose, even though we are of diverse nationalities, cultures, and worship traditions.

Jesus Christ believed that His Church could be one. He prayed that we would. It is my hope and prayer that this book will help Christ's Church

realize His belief and answer His prayer.
YES WE CAN LOVE ONE ANOTHER!

Warren R. Angel
September, 1996
California

1

The First Century Church as the Model for Our Common Faith

I knew I was in trouble as I watched the *agape* smile on the professor's face turn into a scowl. He looked up from my resume. "Well," he said, almost sneering at me, "I see you've been getting a good dose of Pepperdine's liberal theology!"

Stunned, I could barely utter a protest. "Uh . . . well, no . . ." Pepperdine University? Liberal theology? Yes, some professors there did hold liberal views, but that did not negate their faith in Jesus Christ nor their evangelical orientation. "Pepperdine's religion department isn't liberal," I muttered.

Hostility remained in his eyes. "What do you consider yourself theologically?" I knew what he was after. He wanted to categorize me into some theological pigeonhole to prove to himself that I was a liberal trying to sneak onto the faculty of an evangelical school. I realized the interview was over. But I knew I'd feel better by stating the truth — even if he didn't like my answer.

"Actually," I said, staring squarely at him, "I'm just a Christian."

He laughed, shifting uncomfortably, obviously embarrassed at his own question. Of course. Wasn't everybody in the Church supposed to be a Christian?

But he could not let me simply be a Christian because he wasn't sure what that meant anymore. Probably he thought my reply was an evasive answer — which it wasn't. My honesty made him even more suspicious. Pepperdine and I were already compartmentalized in his mind, a tragic result of the polarization and disunity in the Church.

We went through the motions of an interview for a few minutes, and then he said, "We'll keep your application on file."

I knew what that meant.

On the way home I was more angry than disappointed. Evidently the teaching position wasn't something God wanted me to have, and that was okay.

But I was angry because a fellow Christian never sought to understand me or even listen to me. False information had caused him to judge me wrongly. What kind of Christianity was that?

Would Jesus have judged me falsely? Would Paul?

Whatever happened to the first century Church?

Because I knew the answer to the question, I realized I couldn't entirely blame the professor for his lack of Christian charity. Through centuries of history, the modern Church has, in many ways, distanced itself from the Church of Christ and the apostles, the Church founded in the faith, love, and blood of men and women who cherished the common bond of salvation they held together through the saving grace of Jesus Christ.

We have become quite unlike Christ and His Church, especially in the matter of divisions, in the continual fragmenting of the Church. There is, of course, nothing inherently wrong with being Baptist, Methodist, Catholic, or anything else in Christ's Church. The problem arises when we take sides by refusing to understand and accept one another, by insisting that our way is superior to someone else's tradition. Today there is so much suspicion and distrust of anyone who doesn't belong to our own denomination or cherish our theological presuppositions that we've all become quick to judge and slow to accept.

Yet some in Christ's Church *are* working to

recapture that commonality of faith exhibited by the early Church. In March of 1994 forty evangelical Protestant and Catholic scholars and leaders drafted a document stating their intentions to work closely together as brothers and sisters in Christ, especially in the cause of Christian mission. Entitled *Evangelicals and Catholics Together: The Christian Mission in the Third Millennium,* the signers included Charles Colson, founder of Prison Fellowship, and Avery Dulles of Fordham University. The document has also been endorsed by a number of Protestant leaders and Catholic bishops.

Sadly, many Protestants have ignored or criticized this new effort of love and cooperation, notably John MacArthur, Jr., a pastor and president of The Master's College in Newhall, California. A prolific author, MacArthur believes that Catholicism is a heresy and that Catholics are on their way to hell. Conversion to his brand of Christianity is their only hope.

Catholics should not feel singled out for MacArthur's wrath. He also dislikes Protestants who disagree with him. In his book *The Gospel According to Jesus,* he criticized several professors at Dallas Theological Seminary for holding views on salvation he considered contrary to the teachings of Jesus.

The reality is that John MacArthur, Jr., has little love for anyone—*and this is quite contrary to the gospel according to Jesus!* He deliberately and steadfastly perpetuates the disunity of Christ's Church, directly against the wishes of Jesus Himself, who prayed that His disciples would be one.

But MacArthur is not alone in his arrogance and disdain for any movement fostering Christian harmony. Kathy, a friend of mine in her fifties, was disowned by her family long ago. Why? Because she left the church of her youth and joined another. "There is no other," her family told her. "They're all going to hell." They will not speak to her to this day.

Many "Kathys" share her sorrows.

Mary is another friend who had a negative experience at the Catholic hospital where she works. She is not allowed to do one thing there she would very much like to do—participate in the Eucharist. Protestants may attend the chapel mass but are prohibited from the Eucharist. This has long been official Catholic doctrine, yet in fact many American priests in particular do allow non-Catholics to partake in the Eucharist, believing that sincere brothers and sisters in Christ should not be excluded.

Mary was so hurt that she wrote Pope John Paul II asking why any Christian should be excluded from the Catholic communion table. She has not received a reply from the Vatican. The pope is a very busy man, I explained to her. No other Christian writes and travels as he does.

Yes We Can Love One Another!

Yet perhaps John Paul II *did* reply! To the surprise of many Catholic leaders, in 1995 he issued an encyclical letter on ecumenism strongly urging the unity of all Christians. Entitled *Ut Unum Sint* (from Jesus' prayer in John 17, "that they may be one"), the pope acknowledges the past sins of some Catholic clergy, and calls upon all Christians to become one in fellowship with God and Christ in the tradition and faith of the apostles.

And Pope John answered the cry of Mary's heart when he said that Catholic ministers may, "in particular cases," administer certain sacraments, including the Eucharist, to non-Catholics. And Catholics also may request the same sacraments from any Christian minister not in full communion with the Catholic Church (see p. 56 of the encyclical booklet published by St. Paul Books & Media).

The winds of change are blowing. The fresh air Pope John XXIII hoped would blow through the Catholic Church by calling Vatican II in the early 1960s is indeed bringing change. Protestants would do well to pray for that same fresh air of the Holy Spirit, who wants to sweep into and through our lives and make us more like our Savior, whom we all claim to love and serve.

We do not have to be an unloving and fragmented Church. Even though history and time have divided Christian from Christian, *we can love and respect one another and appreciate and share the common faith we have in Jesus Christ.*

But if we are to recapture the commonality of love and faith, as well as the purity and intensity of Jesus and the apostles and saints of the first century Church, we will have to once again examine their lives and their message. For the Christ of the New Testament, the Christ who practiced love and forgiveness by eating with sinners and refusing to stone a woman caught in the act of adultery, is not always found in the theology and practices of the modern Church.

But Jesus can always be found in the beauty and power of that first century gospel story. Indeed, it is there the Church of the future will look for Him and come to Him every day.

It is there that Christians of any church — if they open their hearts and minds — will find the *real* Jesus and the *real* Christian way of love, some, perhaps, for the first time.

It all began nearly two thousand years ago when Jesus walked the dusty roads of Palestine teaching the good news of God's love and forgiveness. He shared the possibility of a daily life enriched by faith and righteousness, and the hope of heaven as He journeyed up and down the narrow strip of land drenched with the blood of endless battles throughout history — the land that's being splattered with blood even today.

Jesus visited well-known places like Jerusalem, the holy city, where He was eventually put to death, and Jericho, the ancient town destroyed many times by invading armies but today a modern city called Tell es-Sultan.

He shared the words of faith, hope, and love, and the reality of a near and caring God, often in humble and insignificant villages like Nain, a dot of a town on the slope of the Galilean hills, and Capernaum on the beautiful Sea of Galilee, where He and His family eventually lived. Tiny places long forgotten, yet their approximate sites have been rebuilt and exist today under new names.

The Gospels tell us that people were astonished whenever Jesus opened His mouth to teach. For He, unlike many of the religious leaders of His day, taught with authority. "No man ever spoke like this man!"

It was not only how Jesus spoke, but what He said that startled His hearers.

"You shall love your neighbors as yourself."

"God is spirit, and those who worship him must worship in spirit and truth."

"I am the resurrection and the life; he who believes in me, though he die, yet shall he live, and whoever lives and believes in me shall never die."

But it wasn't only the teachings of Jesus which persuaded people to follow Him, but also His deeds. He was not just a teacher, but a *doer*. He healed the sick and cast out demons, restoring diseased, broken bodies to wholeness and sick, twisted minds to soundness. Skeptics today deny that Jesus did these things—just as the skeptics in Jesus' day denied them! But crowds followed Him everywhere, hundreds thronging to be near Him so that at times He had to withdraw just to avoid being worn like a frayed rope.

Jesus' ministry in the length and breadth of Palestine lasted no more than three years at the most. During that time there was a hard core of believers who followed Him from almost the beginning of His teachings and who persisted even to His death. It was to these, Jesus' closest disciples that He revealed much of His inner thoughts—thoughts about who he was and why God had called Him to a lonely, hard, and at times desperate ministry in the land of Palestine.

After a time, it was of these closest followers that Jesus asked, "Who do men say that the Son of Man is?"

He was referring to Himself, for the news of this powerful figure who had suddenly appeared from Nazareth was raging throughout the country. Few could keep still and not share an opinion about this man who healed the sick and cast out demons—a man of authority yet one who preached love and forgiveness rather than prejudice and condemnation.

The disciples answered Jesus' penetrating question: "Some say John the Baptist, others say Elijah, and others Jeremiah or one of the prophets."

Jesus was not satisfied with any of these opinions. All of these people were dead, John the Baptist having recently been beheaded by Herod, a ruler in Galilee and son of Herod the Great, the deceased madman of Palestine who had murdered members of his own family and had tried to kill the baby Jesus. Jesus was not a resurrected prophet or preacher, but was sent by God in His own right. He wanted to know if His closest followers perceived this, so He asked them a second question.

"But who do you say that I am?"

Simon Peter, Jesus' most impetuous and zealous apostle and the future early leader of the Church, jumped at the chance to respond. "You are the Christ, the Son of the living God."

Peter understood.

Jesus was elated. "Blessed are you, Simon Bar-Jona! For flesh and blood has not revealed this to you, but my Father who is in heaven. And I tell you, you are Peter, and on this rock I will build my church, and the gates of Hades shall not prevail against it" (Matthew 16:13-18).

The Church was born in this proclamation of Jesus Christ, who emphatically stated that *He,* not swords or politics, would build His Church, and nothing would ever stop its growth, not even the very powers of hell itself.

From that day to this, despite violent opposition, the Church has existed as a moving force in the world.

From the stoning of Stephen only a few years after Christ's ascension into heaven, to the shedding of the martyr's blood by the savagery of the sword and the fires of the stake; to the mass butchery by

Muslims and Communists and other religions and ideologies throughout the centuries; to the senseless slaughter of priests, nuns, and missionaries in Latin America in our time, the world has tried to decimate the Church and its message of love and salvation. Even the Church itself has, occasionally and unwittingly, come close to self-destruction.

But Jesus said it would never happen. His words have proven to be true.

Following the death and resurrection of Jesus, the newborn Church began to grow even in the face of a few internal conflicts and sporadic persecution. By the end of the first century, the apostles and disciples—men and women working side by side— had spread the good news of Jesus throughout Palestine and into Asia Minor (modern Turkey), Greece, Italy, and, according to tradition, for the New Testament is silent, even into Egypt, North Africa, Spain, and India.

What was it about the Church of the first century that made it so successful despite widespread opposition caused by its intrusion into cultures of divergent religions and ideologies?

First of all, the message which those bold, apostolic pioneers shared with their world was intensely personal. God was no vague concept or a wood carving or a legal code written on stone. Rather, God was experienced and shared as a *living, loving, forgiving being who knew and cared for people no matter what their social status.* Jesus Christ was not a dead teacher or prophet, but a *living, loving Savior* who promised forgiveness of sins and a blessed, everlasting life that was infinitely better than one's present existence no matter what his or her social circumstances.

Secondly, this new religion, soon to be called "Christian," was not an external system of ritual sacrifice and obligatory, oral assent, but an internal flooding of the mind and spirit with divine love and understanding; an ontological power through the Spirit of God that enabled a person to live a righteous and beneficial daily life even in the midst of an oppressive and immoral society. An indescribable peace and joy came from receiving Christ and from a sense of serving the living God, a peace and joy which could not be taken out of one's heart and being even by torture and ultimate death.

Furthermore, this new religion was characterized by *love.* This divinely-infused love spread like a raging fire, touching everyone in its sight, for Christianity was not an ethnic or caste religion, but universal in scope, a religion which welcomed everyone. The churches of the New Testament were characterized by people of many nationalities and economic levels, worshiping and working together in harmony and love. Jew and Gentile, Greek and Roman, noble and slave, rich and poor: All were one in God's eyes, who loves equally and without distinction. A mark of the true Christian was that he or she did indeed love other people.

Moreover, the early Church understood itself for what it was intended to be: *a spiritual kingdom sharing spiritual truth with a troubled world.* The Church of the first century was not mystical, secretive, or other-worldly. Christianity was understood and experienced as a life-changing religion that affected one's daily activities in every way. But it was first of all a spiritual experience which transformed one's inner being, not by ritual and law, but by God's love and by the very power and presence of His Son, Jesus Christ, through the Holy Spirit.

This is the picture of the Church the New Testament writers paint for us in the first century. It is a Church with some conflicts and imperfections, but nevertheless it is a *single* Church of harmony, love, and beauty. It knows no divisions. There is no Catholic or Orthodox church. There are no Protestant denominations. The young Church knows only that Jesus Christ is its Savior, and its mandate is to share this belief with the world.

But as early as the first half of the second century, deterioration began to gnaw at the very foundations of the Church in three different areas:

1. Individual Christians began to drift away from a true spirituality—a spirituality which sprang from an experiential knowledge of the risen Christ—to return to the "safer" and easier waters of ritual observance and an old religious legalism.

Two Christian documents of the period reflect this trend. *The Didache* is a catalog of liturgical prescriptions not found in the New Testament. The writer is more concerned with form than freedom in the Holy Spirit. And *The Shepherd of Hermas* is a work in the apocalyptic genre whose author demonstrates a preoccupation with sin and repentance.

Although the New Testament is greatly concerned with these themes, it is not preoccupied with them. Both of these works were for a time considered on a par with the New Testament writings.

Once the drift from a true spirituality had begun, divisions began to appear in both the theology and practices of the Church.

2. Also as early as the second century, individual churches began the slide from autonomy to the centralized control of a hierarchical system, a slide that proved to have a devastating effect not only on churches, but on the lives of Christians throughout the Dark Ages and even through the Reformation and on into our time. (Contrary to what they like to think, Protestants have developed many systems of control.)

Writing to the church at Smyrna (a city in modern Turkey) ca. A.D. 100, Ignatius, the bishop of the church at Antioch in Syria, said, "follow the bishop, as Jesus Christ follows the Father . . . Let no one do anything pertaining to the church without the bishop . . . Wherever the bishop appears, there let the congregation be, just as wherever Jesus

Christ is, there the catholic church is. It is not lawful without the bishop either to baptize or to hold a love feast; but whatever he approves, this is also pleasing to God."

In Ignatius' time a bishop was the equivalent of a local pastor or minister, the "head" or overseer of a local church. This office is mentioned by the apostle Paul in Philippians 1:1, 1 Timothy 3:2, and Titus 1:7. In 1 Peter 2:25 Jesus is referred to as a bishop, although the Greek word is often translated "guardian." The office of bishop or pastor of a local congregation was, evidently, instituted by Paul in the mid-first century.

But the bishop of Paul's time was intended to be only an overseer, whereas Ignatius carried the office to that of one who exercised control over his flock. For Ignatius says "it is not lawful" to do certain things without the *presence* of the bishop.

The intentions of Ignatius were godly. The churches of his time were under attack both from without and within. Persecution by the Roman government, though usually sporadic, was bloody and bitter, costing many Christians their lives. And it would continue at the pleasure of the Romans until the time of Constantine in the early fourth century.

Furthermore, as people vied for power and prestige in the local churches, various heretical teachings arose, some of which threatened to tear the new faith asunder. It was in response to this turmoil that Ignatius said "follow the bishop." He trusted the bishops to follow Christ and contend for the faith of the apostles. This they did—and the Church grew even in the midst of persecution and heresy.

Yet toward the end of the second century Irenaeus, the bishop of the church at Lyons (modern France), further appeals to churches to yield to the authority of the bishops inasmuch as they represented an ecclesiastical succession in line with the apostles and their tradition of faith.

Irenaeus was a man of faith in Jesus Christ—one of the great saints of the Church. His monumental work, *Against Heresies,* was written to bolster the teachings of the Church against heretical sects, particularly Gnosticism, a secretive religion which was a syncretism of Christian, Jewish, and Greek thought.

But in his defense of the pure Christian faith he not only pleads for the support of the bishops, but also—and this was a new trend—that "all the churches (that is, the faithful everywhere) must agree with Rome because of its special priority, for those who spread everywhere have maintained in her the tradition received from the apostles."

Later, the church at Rome, having become the head of the Catholic church, would demand obedience and insist that salvation could be found only in her dominion. Irenaeus would have been shocked at this pompous exclusivity and authoritarianism. But he and Ignatius and others, in their honest defense of the Church, inadvertently planted the seeds of movement toward the centralization of Church power. As this trend occurred, divisions were inevitable, for not everyone could accept the primacy of the Roman church.

3. The most devastating problem the Church experienced, even by the end of the first century, was that it began to lose that precious infusion of God's love. We see this happening in the last New Testament book, The Revelation to John, written ca. A.D. 96. The apostle is instructed to write these words to the church at Ephesus, which was undergoing persecution: "I know you are enduring patiently and bearing up for my name's sake, and you have not grown weary. But I have this against you, that you have abandoned the love you had at first" (2:3-4).

Here was a church which was determined to keep its belief in Jesus Christ and which contended for the purity of the gospel. But sometimes in the struggle for one's life and in the contention for one's beliefs love is gradually abandoned and replaced by self-righteousness and arrogance. These attitudes, in turn, often lead to jealousy, anger, strife, and hatred. This was the problem with the church at Ephesus. Love for God and for Christ was forgotten as the believers battled for survival both as human beings and as Christians.

The Church's love continued to dissipate as its struggles continued. Even after persecution against the Church was virtually ended in A.D. 313, the battle for the faith remained. Heresy and dissent sprung up everywhere. Thus, Augustine, one of the Church's great thinkers, felt compelled to write ca. A.D. 400 that it was *perfectly okay to use force against heretics.* Better they should be dragged violently — maybe dead — into the kingdom of God than be cast into hell.

But this is not love. And this is not God's way.

Love began to disappear in another way by the first half of the second century. An increased preoccupation with law, sin, and ritual tells us that the Church was becoming *reflective.* Instead of receiving, experiencing, and sharing God's love with the world, the Church began to focus on itself.

The first century Church focused on its message — Jesus Christ. Jesus had saved them from their sins and had called them to preach this message of salvation to the world. This the Church continued to do. But gradually it began to replace love, concern for others, and a missionary zeal with laws, ritualism, and, soon, even asceticism and monasticism, the latter being the ultimate escape from the world (monasticism did have some redeeming value).

Once love began to evaporate from the thought and lives of Christians, authoritarianism and a lust for power, along with many other negative attitudes and values, crept in. More than any other factor, it was this lack of love which caused the drift away from the spirituality and harmony of the first century Church.

Even to this day love is sometimes hard to find in those who claim to be members of the Church that Christ founded.

Although it is true that the Church of history has drifted from the Church of the first century—at times and in places so far adrift that it cannot be identified with the Church—it is also true that throughout Church history individual Christians have shone brightly through the maze of Christianity. By their dedication to Christ, their understanding of the spiritual nature of the Church, and, in turn, their zeal in ministering to the needs of humanity, these stalwarts of the Church have demonstrated the love and power of Jesus Christ from generation to generation.

Some of their names are familiar.

Polycarp, bishop of Smyrna, who, by refusing to curse Christ because "he has never done me harm," suffered a martyr's violent death in A.D. 156 and became an example for countless thousands who also died for their faith.

Francis of Assisi demonstrated a selfless love in medieval Europe's period of ecclesiastical domination by renouncing his father's wealth (ca. A.D. 1200) to share Christianity with the masses of poor and ignorant peasants.

Martin Luther, who challenged the might of the Catholic Church when he became convinced that its abuses ran contrary to the spirit of the Church's founder, showed a courage that withstood not only the institutionalized power of Rome, but also the doubts and fears of Luther's own heart and faith.

John Wesley was a man of bold faith who bucked the prevailing Protestant teaching of the 1700s, Calvinism, to fervently share the biblical teaching of salvation for *all* who call upon Christ, and to help the sick and the destitute.

We see an unusual dedication and spirituality in a Dutch Roman Catholic lady known only to us as Mrs. Wielmaker (shared with the world by Corrie ten Boom in her book *The Hiding Place*), who, though imprisoned during World War II in Ravensbrück, a Nazi concentration camp for women, risked her life to comfort and uplift the spirits of the broken and battered women around her by sharing the Bible not only in her native Dutch, but also by taking the time and energy to translate the Scriptures into German, French, Latin and Greek.

Through these fearless and loving Christians, the light of the Church, though dim at times, has been carried through history. These names are but a few of those recorded in the history books, saints who are, in reality, neither Catholic nor Protestant, but simply Christian.

History has failed to note thousands upon thousands of others who shared the love and vision of the Church's founder, Jesus Christ. Their faces and names have vanished with the dust of passing time, men and women of faith and courage, saints who often had little knowledge of the first century Church or the Scriptures, yet who looked to God with an open heart and received from the abundance of heaven all of its spiritual treasures.

Why else has the Church survived? Church historian Clyde L. Manschreck points out that the message of the early Christian community, the Church of the New Testament period, has been "abused, institutionalized, abandoned, rationalized" over the centuries.[1]

But the Church is alive—not in perfect health, but alive.

It is not the visible, institutionalized Church which has fulfilled the words of Christ—"I will build my church, and the gates of Hades shall not prevail against it"—but individuals who have experienced the risen Christ and have responded with faith and love.

This brings us to the theme of this study, how those of us in the modern Church, Catholics and Protestants alike, can find love, unity, and purpose in our common faith.

We need to realize, first of all, that we will never find true unity in human institutions. For the Church didn't just happen. It is God's doing. He brought it into existence through Jesus Christ to be a ministering servant to those whom God deeply loves and cares for—people of every color, language, dialect, and nationality.

The Church belongs to God and to Jesus Christ.

Catholic theologian Hans Küng who, ironically, criticized Pope John Paul's recent encyclical letter on unity, gives us an incisive statement about unity in his discourse on the Church:

> The unity of the Church is not simply a natural entity, is not simply moral unanimity and harmony, is not just sociological conformity and uniformity. To judge it by externals (canon law, ecclesiastical language, Church administration, etc.) is to misunderstand it completely. The unity of the Church is a spiritual entity. It is not chiefly a unity of the members among themselves, it depends finally not on itself but on the unity of God, which is efficacious through Jesus Christ in the Holy Spirit . . . It is one and the same confession of faith in the Lord Jesus, the same hope of blessedness, the same love, which is experienced in oneness of heart, the same service of the world. The Church *is* one and therefore *should be* one.[2]

One of the major problems in achieving a spiritual unity is that too many people in the Church cling to misconstrued opinions of the

Church's nature and purpose. In far too many instances, especially on the far right and far left of the theological spectrum, the modern Church has little affinity with the Church of the first century.

In some places, the theological *systems* and *laws* of fundamentalism, many of which are based on faulty exegesis, have become so prevalent and perverse that the mere weight of them stifles the presence and love of Jesus Christ in His own Church. At the opposite extreme, liberalism has become so *negative* by its dogmatic denunciations of biblical history, faith, and theology, that it is driving people away from the Church in droves.

Both of these loveless extremes, and other factors as well, have caused the Church's present fragmentation. This is the same process that began in the second century. But it has increased in rapidity and in volume just as dissensions and conflicts have increased in the world, particularly the last seventy-five years. Writing in the editorial to the book *Polarization in the Church,* Hans Küng and Walter Kasper note, "we cannot be blind to the sad fact that in the Church in recent years, as in society in general, tensions have increased, polarizations have sharpened and conflicts have become more bitter."[3]

In the Church of today it is difficult to find anyone who is, simply, a *Christian.* It is even more difficult to find someone who will let other Church members simply *be* Christian.

Rather, we want to label everyone as *something.* After all, in the modern Church we have not only

Catholics and Protestants, but fundamentalists, liberals, evangelicals, Calvinists, dispensationalists, charismatics, and a few dozen or so other "kinds" of Christians.

Curiously, we often wear our own labels proudly, but the labeling of others is usually done to denote a negative distinction between "them" and "us." Few of us are willing to be as loving and accepting of others as were the Christians of the first century Church.

Some diversification would not be so bad, of course, except that as each new theology or cause or group arises its adherents tend to become exclusive, being firmly convinced in their own minds that they have found the truth and have become God's gift to the world in its terrible hour of need.

For example, two relatively new and radically diverse theologies, Christian reconstructionism among fundamentalists, and liberation theology among liberals, are often equated by their followers with Christianity itself. Many of their respective adherents view those who question their motives and theology as sub-Christian.

This is the stuff that divisions are made of.

The most tragic result of the ongoing fragmentation of the Church is that many people have given up and dropped out confused, disoriented, and disgusted. What **is** the *real* Church? Does it still exist? Or has it faded from history? If it does exist, where is it? Many places simply don't satisfy that spiritual need of believers which the first century Church seemed to fulfill.

The first century Church, after all, understood the stuff that peace and love and harmony are made of:

1. The presence and love of God that ministers life to every human being who is open to Him.

2. Faith in Christ, the one who saves us from our sins and sustains us day by day through the promised Holy Spirit.

3. The insightful study of the Scriptures that enlightens the intellect as well as nurturing the human spirit.

4. The warmth and love and prayers of fellow Christians which comforts and helps us through the daily trials of life.

This is real Christianity—people who care about each other and who diligently minister to the spiritual and physical needs of all human beings.

We can be that Church of the first century, a Church which, though divided by nationality, culture, and custom, was nevertheless a Church united by its belief in Christ Jesus and marked with integrity, spirituality, faith, hope, and love. We can be, *if we want to be,* that same Church, though divided by traditions and practices—and by the name on the door—united by Christ in nature and purpose and by our love for one another.

I am not so critical or blind as to believe that the Church of Jesus and the apostles and disciples does not, in fact, exist today. One of the joys in writing this book is the certain knowledge that the first century Church *does* exist. It exists in the hearts and lives of thousands upon thousands of Christians around the world. It exists in the ministry of thousands of local churches in every country on the face of the earth. It exists behind the names "Catholic" and "Protestant."

Furthermore, it exists wherever Christians of all backgrounds meet together for Bible study, prayer, and for sharing the message of Christ with a lost world. And this is happening in small groups and in mass meetings more often as Christians become conscious of their common faith and are desirous of fellowship and evangelistic cooperation.

Yet the New Testament Church of today is often obscured by the negative attitudes conveyed by people like the professor who falsely accused me without trying to understand me.

If we are going to share our common faith, we will need to understand the genesis and essence of that faith. To that end we will turn in the chapters ahead.

But to truly *be* the Church of Jesus and His disciples, we must desire it. And to desire it we must believe not only that Jesus Christ is our Savior, but that we can never fully be His disciples unless we are the answer to the cry of His heart the night before His crucifixion: "My prayer is not for them alone. I pray also for those who will believe in me through their message, that all of them may be one, Father, just as you are in me and I am in you. May they also be in us so that the world may believe that you have sent me" (John 17:20-21, NIV).

Pope John Paul II, in writing his encyclical letter *Ut Unum Sint* in 1995, longed with thousands of Catholics and Protestants the world over that we might truly be a Church united in Jesus Christ. I pray the Holy Spirit won't rest until *every* Christian desires it!

How can those of us who say we love Jesus Christ *not be* the answer to His prayer? Indeed, we can!

2

Anyone Can Understand the
Church's Book of Faith and History

For several years I was the pastor of an interdenominational church in the Los Angeles area. The congregation included Catholics, Lutherans, Methodists, Presbyterians, and Pentecostals worshiping alongside others who had come to Christ there or at a nearby sister church. This was my first senior pastorate. Normally, even if a minister is scared out of his wits by the prospect of that first church, great things in the Lord are highly anticipated.

The problem was that the "great things" which at first occurred were *not* what I had anticipated!

The previous pastor had ingrained in all those

who would listen to him (a number of people left the church) a doctrinal teaching commonly referred to as *submission*. The basic idea is that a woman is to obey her husband implicitly, for he is the head of the family. A wife is not to seek God for anything of importance since her husband stands between her and Christ and will tell her all she needs to know and direct her in all she is to do. There are many facets to this teaching, some of which involve sex. Very little of it is found in Scripture and is, in fact, contrary to Scripture.

I was aware that the previous pastor had taught this, but I was not in the least prepared for the depth in which this teaching had been implanted.

"Would you steal a steak at the supermarket if your husband told you to?" I asked one young woman.

"Absolutely!" she responded without hesitation. "If my husband tells me to do something, it's as though Christ Himself is telling me." (Fortunately, this particular husband would not have told his wife to do that.)

Not only did this teaching affect the way these people lived, but it developed in them an attitude of religious superiority over those who didn't believe it. One day I was sharing the Scriptures with one of the submission believers. I wasn't sure I was making progress. That was confirmed when he finally yelled at me in frustration. "Look," he said, "I don't care if you have one hundred verses to my one, I'm never going to believe what you're telling me!"

As far as I know I never did make any progress with the hard-liners. Even though I shared the truth with them as God led me to do, they all eventually left the church. To this day I can only hope that either my words or those of someone else turned their hearts and minds to the truth.

There were others in the congregation who accepted what good they found in the submission teaching and rejected the rest. They stayed because Christ was first in their lives and because they loved their church. I enjoyed their fellowship and support.

But the hard-liners gnawed at me day and night. I often asked myself and God the same question as I sought Him in prayer: Why can't Christians understand the Bible?

Since those weary days in the early 1970s, I've learned many reasons why understanding the Bible is a difficult task for more than a few Christians. Sometimes understanding is limited by our attitudes toward the Bible. For other people, the ways in which the Bible is taught and presented is so stifling that it not only stagnates Christian growth, but also contributes to divisions among Christians by fostering negative attitudes. Once these views of the Bible, the Church, or any particular theology are perceived as "truth," one's mind automatically sets up a barrier against any conflicting information, and hostility against those who teach it.

This is what happened to those who became enmeshed in the submission teaching. Even though I tried to treat them fairly and minister to them as I did other members of the congregation, a few of them openly despised me because I didn't agree with their teachings.

This is why a good understanding of the Bible is so important. I don't mean to imply that Christians need to agree on everything written in the Bible in order to share our common faith. But the Bible is the Church's book of faith and history. Agreement on basic Christian teaching is essential to Christian fellowship.

Can we do this? Can Protestants ever agree with one another and with Catholics on the basic message of our handbook?

For some people this will mean coming to a new understanding of the Bible. Can we change our minds about the Bible's teachings? Do people change their minds? *Absolutely!*

But it's not always easy. Sometimes God has to shake us up before we can look at the Bible objectively.

After I'd left the pastorate in Los Angeles to work on a master's degree at Pepperdine University, I settled in teaching a young married couple's class at a large church while working part-time for Youth With A Mission.

At the church I was surprised to run into an old boyhood friend of mine. He'd found the Lord, married, been widowed, married again, and matured into a level-headed Christian. This was not the boy I used to know, although I remembered that his father was a saintly man who read the Scriptures and prayed every day—often for his son.

I was surprised when my friend shared with our Sunday school class his deliverance from a mind-bending "Christian" commune.

This is another form the submission teachings take, when an individual sets himself up as some sort of "shepherd" over others, an absolute authority who tells his followers how to live.

My friend and his first wife somehow got involved, even though doubts plagued his mind. One day he caught the leader slapping his wife around. Immediately the darkness began to lift from his brain. For the first time he could hear the Spirit speaking to his heart. They left the commune the next day, and after that he studied the Bible as if it were a new book.

Sometimes God opens our minds through the efforts of other people. Such was the situation with the Church's greatest reformer, Martin Luther. If it weren't for his superior, Johann von Staupitz, vicar of the Augustinian order, Luther might never have read the Scriptures. In the sixteenth century Catholic Church, the Bible was not always studied as the Word of God by those entering the priesthood. This is the tragic situation among some Protestant seminarians today.

Even though Luther was a priest, he could find no peace in his soul. He was obsessed with confessing non-existent sins, certain that God was angry with him, ready to condemn him to hell. Staupitz grew tired of listening to his ridiculous confessions and told him: "Man, God is not angry with you. You are angry with God. Don't you know that God commands you to hope?"[4]

Staupitz was a priest who did know the Scriptures. And knowing that they held the key to life, to peace and rest and assurance in the God of salvation, Staupitz assigned Luther to teach the Bible at the University of Wittenberg.

Luther protested, realizing he didn't know the Bible, but to no avail. Staupitz insisted. Luther now had no choice but to study the Bible, perhaps for the first time in his life.[5] When he did, the power of the Scriptures, the reality of God's love, and the sufficiency of Christ's death in securing forgiveness for him—personally—gradually took root in his heart and spirit. Prayer, fasting, penance, confession, hard work—none of these things helped Luther. It was the Word of God that changed not only his theology, but his life.

The foregoing illustrations demonstrate not only the positive side of Bible study, but also the negative. For while it is encouraging to know that minds and lives can be opened to God's Word, their stories prompt a question that needs to be examined: Why were Christian minds closed to the

Bible in the first place?

In the case of my boyhood friend, his first encounter with the Bible was not a serious study of the Scriptures themselves, but a learning experience under a dogmatic, fundamentalist teaching which was imposed *upon* the Scriptures. The submission teaching is not new and has been taught over the years in various places including Catholic communities, Baptist, Christian, and charismatic churches. The extremes of this teaching vary widely. But one facet of it never varies: The doctrine of submission in its totality is a theological system thrown over the entire Bible, especially the New Testament, thereby making all other theologies subservient to it.

Adherents claim that this is not true, but in actuality the submission doctrine dominates everything they do and say.

This is true of many other teachings as well. Dispensationalism, for example, which also contains some truth, has been for many the *only* theological system of interpretation for several decades. (This complicated theology was invented in the 1830s and popularized more recently by the Scofield Bible.)

Curtis Crenshaw, a Presbyterian minister and an adherent of dispensationalism for thirty-one years, comments on his failure to understand the Bible because dispensationalism was imposed so tightly upon it: "I distinctly missed the unity of the Bible in God's covenant of grace in Christ. My unifying element in theology — whether systematic or biblical —

was eschatology, by which standard all dispensationalists tested the orthodoxy of others."[6]

Another example is that of the health and wealth gospel, or prosperity gospel (some call it "name-it-claim-it" or "positive confession"), taught by a number of so-called charismatic teachers. This is another theological system thrown over the whole of Scripture.

The key to health and wealth, we are told, is faith. The unlocking of that faith is a positive utterance of words. These two little yet powerful keys to understanding the Bible will make a Christian healthy, wealthy, and certainly wise. Those who fail to utilize faith and the power of the tongue are not only going to lose out on God's blessings, but they're not really living the Christian life.

What these teachers try to convey is that God has subjected human beings to a whole set of spiritual laws. Once we plug into these laws we can receive all of God's blessings. The problem is that their "spiritual laws" ignore or distort much of what the Bible really says. They're also illogical.[7]

The effect on people who have gobbled up this teaching like kids inhaling candy has often been devastating. Some have died by refusing to see a doctor. Others have grown bitter toward God because the promised blessings never arrived.

God gave us the Bible that it might minister *life.*

Theological systems don't minister life. They produce little more than a cadre of adherents who live and breathe their systems while failing to understand and thereby receive the benefits of God's Word.

The Bible is a big book. There's a lot more in it than one narrow and often poorly-focused theological system.

The case of Martin Luther demonstrates another reason why understanding the Bible can be difficult. He didn't think he needed to study the Bible.

The reason for this is not clear, but it is true that the Bible had become somewhat of a dormant book in the Catholic Church of Luther's day. This was only generally true, however, because Luther's superior, Staupitz, was a student and scholar of the Bible. Luther probably reasoned that, being a priest, he didn't really need to study the Bible since he already knew everything the Church taught. To his astonishment, when he finally did study the Bible, he discovered that the Scriptures were often at odds with his perception of Christianity.

Martin Luther's problem with biblical knowledge is one often encountered today. Too many Christians are dependent upon *someone else* to tell them what to believe. Even priests and ministers fall into this trap by letting their church's traditional beliefs substitute for their own prayerful Bible study. Or, as often happens, the theology of some long gone giant of the tradition becomes one's theology. There is little effort to study the Bible for oneself to discover whether or not the old traditions measure up to Scripture.

Fundamentalists like to think they don't do this, but they freely cite the works of esteemed theologians and Bible scholars of years long gone to authenticate their "scriptural" beliefs.

This is not to say that the older theologians shouldn't be read. I have many of their books in my own library. But no book is a substitute for God's Word.

Neither are particular traditions, as Luther discovered, nor the writings of present-day ministers and teachers to be used as a substitute for God's Word.

If we are to understand the Bible as its writers and God intended, it is necessary to lay aside biases and ingrained, erroneous ideas about the Bible and its message. I know people, ministers, scholars, and laity alike, who are not willing to do this, not even whey they know the truth. This is tragic, not only for the damage it does to their own lives, but for the harm it sometimes does to others.

Some people think that this is impossible, anyway, that we cannot approach the Scriptures without a bias, no matter how minimal it might be.

Nonsense. God gave each of us a brain and a will—the essential tools for studying the Bible. If He thinks we can learn His ways we should never short-change ourselves by claiming it can't be done.

There is another major hindrance to understanding the Bible among Christians, and this is the view of liberalism that the ancient book is merely man's writing and man's religion. It sees God's direct intervention in history and the miracles in the Bible as either legend or literary invention, and the New Testament as the Church's way of theologizing and creating its very existence.

Liberalism's view of Jesus Christ is particularly devastating for anyone attempting to study His life. Some still see Him as Albert Schweitzer's Jesus, a historical figure to be sure, but nothing more than a deluded Jewish apocalyptic who thought the earthly reign of the kingdom of God would occur in His lifetime. Others agree with Rudolf Bultmann that the Jesus of the New Testament is the apostle Paul's invention, little more than a redeemer myth borrowed from Greek Gnostic writers.

A more recent revision of Christ is that of the Jesus Seminar and other faithless academicians. These pseudo New Testament scholars accept so little of the Gospels as history that they fictionalize Jesus into utter nonsense.

These attitudes discourage serious study of the Bible, especially the New Testament. After all, who in the modern world wants to believe in a conceptualized, mythical figure of the first century Church's faith?

For liberalism—at least for those who strongly adhere to the foregoing—the Bible has become little more than ancient religious literature to be read briefly in worship services. There is nothing certain or absolute in its pages although it does contain some wisdom applicable to our time.

The basic problem with those who share liberalism's view of the Bible is their acceptance of its evaluation by modern science. Since it contains many supernatural elements contrary to scientific history, it must be dismissed as myth or, at best, the exaggeration of its authors.

What liberalism fails to appreciate is the Bible's claim to be a book of *faith.* The biblical writers were not interested in history *per se,* but only as it related to God and mankind's faith in him. This is not to say that biblical history is inaccurate. Indeed, over the past one hundred and fifty years the archaeologist's shovel has proven biblical history to be highly accurate.

The biblical writers were simply honest and intelligent people who never questioned the existence of God. Rather, they wrote what they had heard, experienced, and believed to be true: the *fact* of God's intervention in the affairs of human beings.

The problem with too many of us living in the scientific age is that we demand the answers to things we know little or nothing about. It is not possible, however, to scientifically analyze God, someone we cannot even see. God requires that we approach Him in faith, believing, just as the biblical writers did, that He exists and that He will help us in the daily struggles of life. As the writer of Hebrews says, "Now faith is the assurance of things hoped for, the conviction of things not seen. For by it the men of old received divine approval" (11:1-2).

The beauty of faith is that *God can be believed and experienced.* This is what the Bible is all about. God wants men and women to worship Him and experience Him so that we might have a better life, and eternal life as well.

And when we experience God, just as the men and women of old experienced Him, we don't have to see Him to know that He exists and that the biblical writings really do witness to the fact of His love and care.

Those who disregard the Bible for what it claims to be — or study it with faulty presuppositions — cannot receive it as a book of faith or take it seriously in any way. It becomes for them little more than another relative "history" book.

Liberalism's devaluing of Scripture has long had a negative effect on churches and seminaries. I spent several years at the Graduate Theological Union, a consortium of seminaries in Berkeley, California, commonly known as the GTU. Notoriously liberal, the school has a number of excellent language programs and some good biblical studies. Their library is outstanding.

It was my experience, however, that many instructors, both Catholic and Protestant, didn't believe much of the Bible even though they taught it. A friend of mine at the Presbyterian seminary scrupulously avoided one professor because he tired of hearing him say, "Well, this is what the text (New Testament) says, but, of course, we know that's not true." Another friend dropped out of the Pacific School of Religion when he was literally laughed out of class for sharing his belief in Christ's resurrection. That's just a symbol, he was told.

The real tragedy is that some students meekly accept the negative view of the Bible they find at the GTU and other seminaries and then go out to pastor churches with very little if any faith in the book.

Not all GTU instructors held a negative view of the Scriptures during the time I was there. Furthermore, it was my pleasure to discover many instructors who were open not only to serious Bible study, but also to the viewpoints and fellowship of Christians of varying traditions. John Keating, S.J., professor at the Jesuit School of Theology (currently he is book review manager for the journal *Theological Studies)*, was one such instructor.

I knew that Professor Keating and I didn't hold all theological views in common. But I respected him for his knowledge, genuineness, and for his interest in his students as individuals. He respected me as a serious student, encouraged me in every academic pursuit, and, most importantly, allowed me the freedom to study the Scriptures.

Freedom to study the Scriptures holds the promise of understanding them. If our minds are not free we can never truly study the Bible for what it claims to be—*the inspired Word of God.*

The freeing of our minds opens us to studying the Bible for its historical, theological, and spiritual value, neither imposing doctrinal systems upon it, nor discounting its integrity. This is the view held by many Bible scholars, priests, ministers, and lay persons alike, even in this technical age, who get little press because they are too busy serving Christ by serving their fellow human beings.

These are the people who have discovered a few wondrous things about this old book:

The Bible is the Church's book of *God's love.*

The Bible is the Church's book of *comfort.*

The Bible is the Church's book of *conduct.*

The Bible is the Church's book of *spiritual power.*

The Bible is the Church's book of *inspiration.*

The Bible is the Church's book of *hope.*

The Bible is the Church's book of *faith.*

One of the major causes of sexual abuse among both Catholics and Protestants is that sexual predators either have never read the Bible, don't believe it, or just don't care what it says. They are pretenders in their position as ministers or priests, for the power of Christ and the instruction in the Bible to God's way of living is absent in their lives.

When someone devalues the Scriptures, whether minister, priest, or lay person, they devalue not only God, but themselves, for God gave us His Word that we might live a better and blessed life. He did this because He created us and He loves us.

When someone devalues the Scriptures, they miss out on its *power* to change their lives—the power of Christ and the power of the Holy Spirit.

The power of the Word of God itself.

Whenever and wherever we are open to it, God comes to us through His Word, speaking to our hearts and minds and changing us to conform to the image of Christ, to people of love and goodness and righteousness.

God does not do this for just a few select persons, for His book is the property of anyone who wishes to read it. Though we have many versions of the Bible, it is not a Catholic book, a Protestant book, nor the property of those who claim to have a superior understanding of its content.

All those who treasure the Bible as the inspired Word of God have one mandate: As servants of Christ, Catholic and Protestant brothers and sisters sharing a common faith, we need to study the Bible with open hearts and minds so that we might in turn minister to our world and bring faith and hope and love to needy hearts and lives.

Whenever and wherever we do this, we are no longer Catholic or Protestant. We are simply Christians, people with oneness of heart and purpose.

3

The Christ of the New Testament Is Our Source of Spiritual Power and Contentment

Although my calling as a servant of Christ is not that of an evangelist, I do preach evangelistic sermons from time to time. On one of those occasions, God called upon me to share a few thoughts on Jesus' promise to set us free from the enslaving powers of sin as related in the eighth chapter of the Gospel of John.

While I was sharing these words of a new and better life, I noticed a young lady sitting off to the side of the sanctuary. She looked at me infrequently, and her eyes were hard and bitter. It didn't appear that she believed much of what I was saying—if she was even listening.

After the service, she hung around at the tail end

of those who responded to the altar call. She found her chance to talk to me and approached with defiance written all over her face.

"You seem to think it's easy to conquer sin," she said, half sneering. "But it's not. I've tried and tried. It's not easy at all."

Despite her negative attitude toward both her problem and me, I sensed that she really wanted help. I also realized that she needed in-depth counseling, so my wife and I invited her to our home to talk and to pray. She accepted.

Once we sat down at home and began to share, the defiance left the lady's face. In its place was a mixture of sadness and a plea for help. Sin had become habitual, she confessed. She wanted to stop, but she couldn't. The problem was that she was no longer an active Christian. She wanted to become the Christian she once was, but her life was given over to her habit of sin.

We talked awhile, then we prayed for her. Nothing happened. There was no apparent outward change in her, although she was repentant.

A week later she called. Still nothing had happened. The desire for sin was still strong in her even though she had repented. She wanted to change, she reaffirmed, but just wasn't able to.

We invited her to our house again, and as we prayed the Holy Spirit revealed the answer to her problem. The hindrance in her life was not any weakness of Christ or of prayer--and it was not the devil's stranglehold on her, either. The lady was simply hanging on to that desire for sin. The spiritual side of her knew it was wrong and could not tolerate it. But her flesh clung to it.

When I mentioned this to her she at first denied it. But she paused and looked back on her way out the door. "Well," she said thoughtfully, "maybe you're right."

Several days later she called on the phone. This time her whole being was ready to cast aside her sin. She came over and my wife and I prayed with her again. This time it happened. A floodgate opened from within her, she rededicated her life to Christ, and the power and joy of the Spirit literally overwhelmed her. Not only did her demeanor change, but her life changed. She went on to become one of the most successful persons in her career field and soon became a new bride.

This lady's story is not unique. Thousands of people of every generation all over the world, from drug addicts to murderers, to inveterate gossips and bigots, have experienced this power of Jesus Christ. Any one who *wills* to be free from sin and invites Christ into his or her life can have His power.

Some sociologists and psychologists say that a person's will has little or nothing to do with their actions. While it is true that environmental influences, especially during childhood and young adult years, shape a person's thoughts and attitudes, behaviorists know little about the power of God.

One's will and the power of Jesus Christ are greater than any environmental influence. *No one has to be a slave to negative and destructive thoughts and actions.*

This isn't just my conclusion. Long ago, the apostle Paul came to the same conclusion based on his personal experience of Christ and his observations of others. He reminds the congregation at Corinth, Greece:

> Do you not know that the wicked will not inherit the kingdom of God? Do not be deceived: Neither the sexually immoral nor idolaters nor adulterers nor male prostitutes nor homosexual offenders nor thieves nor the greedy nor drunkards nor slanderers nor swindlers will inherit the kingdom of God. And that is what some of you were. But you were washed, you were sanctified, you were justified in the name of the Lord Jesus Christ and by the Spirit of our God (1 Cor. 6:9-11, NIV).

Corinth was a notoriously evil city in Paul's day. Yet many of these people changed both their habits and their lives through the love and power of Jesus Christ.

What is it about this man Jesus, who taught and ministered in first century Palestine? How is it that He has the power to help humanity change their lives? How is it that in this carpenter's son from tiny Nazareth of Galilee, people of all nationalities, times, and locales can find forgiveness of sin, power to live a righteous life, and receive eternal life?

Why is Jesus Christ any better or any different from other great religious or moral teachers and philosophers, or even from the many great political and social leaders the world has known? Why does Christ have such great spiritual power today?

Although Jesus was born a human being like anyone else, the difference between He and others is that He is God's real son, not merely an earthly son in the sense that all people are God's sons and daughters. Vincent Taylor sees in the biblical title "Son of God" a description of Jesus' relationship to God, not in a spiritual sense, but in the sense of kinship as the word "son" would indicate a blood relationship among physical beings.[8]

As a human being, God's Son shared the very nature and love of the Father with the world. That was Jesus' reason for being.

The nine New Testament authors, who did not all know each other, shared this conviction about Jesus, that He was indeed the divine Son of God and the one who gives to men and women a better life in this world and eternal life in the next.

It was not by collusion that the New Testament authors wrote, but *because of their common experiences and perceptions of this man Jesus.* They believed He was God's real son because in

Him there was power to forgive sins, to heal sick bodies and sick minds, and power to live a holy, righteous, and better life.

We should not suppose, however, that because their consensus concerning Jesus Christ was based on their personal experiences that they did not engage in any research or reflection. To assert, as some do, that the early disciples were a bunch of dumb sheep blindly following Jesus does not do justice either to the capabilities of the human mind, or to the written historical records.

The New Testament writers freely tell us of many who scoffed at the teachings of Jesus and the subsequent preaching of His disciples. Some of these scoffers, notably the apostle Paul, later changed their minds. Undeniably, Paul's encounter with the risen Christ (Acts 9:1-31) played a large role in his conversion. But a change of mind indicates reflection. While Paul was vigorously persecuting the young Church, he was also reflecting on the reports and claims concerning this man many believed was the Christ.

But however much rationalization played a part in forming the views of Jesus held by the writers of the New Testament, their affirmations of Christ came about largely through their experiences of Him. Unlike most modem glitzy advertisements, *Jesus delivered on His promises.* He brought peace, joy, love and hope into their lives. He helped them kick sinful habits and transformed them into persons of righteousness and love. He imparted to them wisdom and help with the daily struggles of life. He encouraged them to have faith in themselves, in God, and in the hope of heaven. He gave them the power to *be* something in the one life God grants everyone.

The New Testament writers believed that Jesus Christ was God's Son and their savior not because they saw the need to invent a new religion or because they wanted to keep His memory alive, but because Christ had made a spiritual and practical difference in their lives.

Indeed, Jesus has made a difference in the lives of all who have truly believed in Him and honestly followed Him throughout the centuries.

Yet it seems that many people in today's Church are not satisfied with the Christ of the New Testament. Quite varied and even astounding opinions are voiced as to who Jesus was.

Debate about the Church's founder is nothing new. Throughout its history the Church has often argued long and loud over the nature of Jesus. Faced with dissent and heresy, Church councils were sometimes called just to discuss whether Jesus was human or divine.

The most notable of these was the Council of Chalcedon in A.D. 451. This gathering of over six hundred bishops accepted the beliefs of the New

Testament writers that Jesus Christ was "truly God and truly man."

This decision has held among most Catholics and Protestants to this day, yet many within both groups are not satisfied with this view of Christ and think it is necessary to add or detract from it.

On the one hand, there are those in the Church who dogmatize Christ into a realm beyond the New Testament understanding of Jesus. One reason for this is the insistence that Christ must be defended against the attacks of unbelief, and so doctrines about Him are fine-tuned until He becomes too wondrous to be the Savior who lives in our hearts. The assertions run something to the effect that Jesus was a literal God-man, capable of doing miracles through His own power and at His own will.

Yet the New Testament never makes these claims. The apostle Peter, in fact, told the first Gentile converts that "God anointed Jesus of Nazareth with the Holy Spirit and with power; he went about doing good and healing all that were oppressed by the devil, for God was with him" (Acts 10:38).

On the other hand, there are those in the Church, as pointed out in Chapter Two, who claim that the Gospel narratives cannot be trusted as history because their picture of Christ is the product of an imaginary faith. This assertion is based solely on the presupposition that the New Testament is an unscientific and therefore non-historic and unreliable collection of documents. The New Testament Jesus is just too supernatural for the intellectualism and sophistication of the modern world, and so the reality of the Christ who miraculously healed the sick, rose from the grave, and saved people from their sins is denied.

The problem with this negative view of Christ and the genesis of the Church is that it denies God's interaction with human beings. The *divine reality* in a person's life is neither understood nor expected. Those who hold to this view have little faith in the God of the Bible — and no faith in the Christ of the New Testament.

The truth about the Jesus of the Gospels lies somewhere between the above two extremes. He is neither too wondrous and mythical to comprehend, nor too supernatural to be believed.

Furthermore, Jesus Christ *is* the common faith of the Church, of all who would profess to be Christian. There can be no real sharing of our faith where there is no basic agreement as to who Jesus was when He walked our earth, and that He is still the life of the Church today.

Where the Christ of the New Testament is shared by all who hold a common faith in Him, there is joy and love and peace one with another, for we all share the commonality of finding in Christ the one who satisfies our spiritual longings.

However, to understand Christ is to first believe with the men and women of both the Old and New Testaments that God exists, that He cares for us, and that He will reach out to help us when we seek His love and care.

The Christians of the first century Church believed that Jesus was sent to be the Savior of the world by the God of the Old Testament. The divine reality they experienced in Christ did not surprise them because they expected God to intervene in their lives.

For these bold, world-changing people of faith, Jesus was neither a doctrine to be believed nor a fable of inventive minds. Rather, He was a living experience of the reality of God. This personal experience of God through Jesus was all the proof they needed that He was indeed the Savior.

Some people detest this sort of subjectivity because personal experience cannot be batted about in the processes of thought nor stuffed into one's computer. But Jesus did not come to earth as a philosophical concept or a computer printout. He came as a human being with the sole purpose of bringing mankind closer to God, to help us understand God and experience Him in a new and real way.

This, basically, is what the New Testament writers tell us about Christ. The writer of Hebrews makes it clear that since we are flesh and blood, Jesus Himself "likewise partook of the same nature."

As God's servant, Jesus did this for two reasons:

1.   "that through death he might destroy him who has the power of death, that is, the devil."

2.   "he had to be made like his brethren in every respect, so that he might become a merciful and faithful high priest in the service of God, to make expiation for the sins of the people. For because he himself has suffered and been tempted, he is able to help those who are tempted" (2:14-18).

These are precious thoughts. Jesus became like us in order to die for our sins and to understand us in our sufferings and temptations.

Was the writer of Hebrews satisfied with the Christ who was told to him by the apostles (2:3-4)? Immensely! For him the words of Jesus proved to be true: "I am the bread of life; he who comes to me shall not hunger, and he who believes in me shall never thirst" (John 6:35).

Jesus Christ satisfies that spiritual hunger and thirst because He comes into one's life and fills it up with the very love and presence of God and helps us live a better and more fulfilling life. This doesn't mean that we won't have problems, but that life will be better because of God's presence and help.

Perhaps no writer expresses his contentment with Christ better than Paul, who wrote thirteen New Testament books. "I have been crucified with Christ; it is no longer I who live, but Christ who lives in me; and the life I now live in the flesh I live by faith in the Son of God, who loved me and gave himself for me" (Galatians 2:20).

Paul had come to know Christ as "the image of the invisible God" (Colossians 1:15), the very reflection of the God Paul served and experienced day by day.

Nothing in all of Paul's letters comes close to his profound comparison of Christ with religious laws and rituals in Colossians. He observes concerning such religious legalism: "These are a shadow of the things that were to come; the reality, however, is found in Christ" (2:16-17, NIV).

As children many of us tried to grab a shadow. Soon we realized the futility of our efforts. As adults many of us tried to depend upon religious laws and rituals for spiritual satisfaction—just as Paul once did.

But the pursuit of laws and rituals always ends in futility, for they leave an emptiness in one's heart and soul that only the experience of Jesus Christ can satisfy.

For Jesus Christ *is* the divine reality in any genuine spiritual experience. This was not the experience of Paul and the writer of Hebrews alone, but of all the New Testament writers:

1. Matthew saw Jesus as a great teacher and a friend of sinners.

2. Mark proclaimed Jesus as the Son of God, great in compassion, who heals bodies, minds, and souls.

3. Luke loved Him as a friend of women, and

one who brings joy to the world by bringing salvation to people everywhere.

4. John described Jesus with varying terms, but most of all knew Him to be the light of the world and the bread of life.

5. James experienced Him as the Lord of glory.

6. Peter, who traveled the dusty roads of Palestine with Jesus yet denied Him three times, later referred to Him as the Shepherd and Guardian of our souls.

7. Jude served Christ as his Master and Lord, full of love and mercy.

This is the Christ of the first century Church.

And this is the Christ of our modern period, the Son of God who still brings good things to those who believe in Him. He gives us peace, joy, wisdom, and strength to cope with the most bitter situations. He gives us faith and courage to carry on when our senses beg us to give up. Most of all, Christ assures us that God is with us simply because He loves us and cares for us.

Despite all the loving praise to Christ in the New Testament by those who had discovered in Him a precious fountain of salvation, many people in our modern age of science and technology stumble over the death of Christ. It makes no sense to them that God would sacrifice His own Son on behalf of others, or that the death of a human being could in any way bring about the forgiveness of sin.

One reason for the failure to understand the

death of Christ is that it is not always seen as *God's redeeming love.* But it cannot properly be viewed as anything else. In its fullest expression, from both the point of God and the actions of Jesus, His death was an act of love.

For God's ultimate purpose in sending His own Son to the earth—rather than calling someone already on the earth to be His emissary—was that we might see Him through Christ and so experience His love.

Sometimes love reaches its greatest height in death, just as it did in Christ's death. We need only to look at life around us to see how true this is. A mother or father will often make a desperate attempt to save a child from a burning home. Sometimes neither is able to escape the smoke and the flames.

Northern California coastal waters are extremely rough and treacherous. It is not uncommon for fishermen or sightseers to be swept off the rocks by sudden high waves. Family members or friends, often without even caring about the danger to their own lives, will jump into the churning waters after them. Sometimes neither is able to escape the relentless pounding of the surf.

The San Francisco-Santa Cruz earthquake of October, 1989, produced a whole horde of heroes who gave no thoughts to the high probability of their deaths as they entered collapsed and tottering buildings and freeways to rescue the missing and those whose cries for help they could no longer ignore—people they didn't even know.

None of these rescuers lost their lives, although wood and concrete could have easily crushed them.

This exceptional demonstration of love is what we see in Christ when He willingly died for us. Paul tells us:

> While we were still weak, at the right time Christ died for the ungodly. Why, one will hardly die for a righteous man— though perhaps for a good man one will dare even to die. But God shows his love for us in that while we were yet sinners Christ died for us (Rom. 5:6-8).

There is agreement among orthodox Catholics and Protestants that Christ's death was an *atoning sacrifice* for the sins of human beings. This is how Jesus' death was understood by the New Testament writers. It was a sacrifice in the mode of an Old Testament animal sacrifice. As Paul told the Corinthian church: "Christ, our paschal lamb, has been sacrificed" (1 Cor. 5:7).

The problem for many people today is that the concept of a blood sacrifice is odious to the modem mind. However, it was not odious to the first century mind. Almost all ancient cultures practiced some sort of animal sacrifice as a means of worshiping a deity. The practice predates Hebraic history, but it is also a significant part of the Mosaic Law. In brief, the slaying of an animal as an act of worship was a means of atoning for one's sins.

We need to bear in mind, however, that the ritual itself meant nothing to God unless those for whom the sacrifice was offered were truly repentant. The writer of Proverbs warned:

> The sacrifice of the wicked is an
> abomination to the Lord, but the prayer
> of the upright is his delight (15:8).

Seen in this light, that Christ came into a world which sacrificed animals, even being born into the religion of Judaism which practiced it as a customary means of worship, Jesus' sacrificial death becomes more understandable.

However, several observations concerning Christ's death as an atoning sacrifice must be kept in mind:

1. The offering was made not by man, but by *God Himself.* Furthermore, Jesus willingly gave His life for us—His friends (John 10:17-18 and 15:13-14).

2. It was *not* a true animal sacrifice according to Old Testament law. These were to be either burned or eaten following their slaughter. But God had no intention of leaving Jesus Christ in the grave. On the third day following His death, God restored Him to life. Soon He ascended to heaven to return to His Father.

Jesus' early disciples, who at first did not believe He had risen from the grave, soon came to understand His restoration to life as inseparable from His death. The resurrection was not only a sign of God's power and proof that Jesus was indeed the divine Savior, but also a visual demonstration that those who believe in Christ will also one day be resurrected from the dead.

3. In Christ's sacrificial death, the need for any animal sacrifice has come to a *permanent end.* The writer of Hebrews discusses this fact at some length. Jesus' death was not like the offerings made by the priests of Israel under the Old Testament system of law, he says, for these had to be offered continually as an expression of repentance and a means of forgiveness. Rather, Christ "has appeared once for all at the end of the age to put away sin by the sacrifice of himself" (9:26). Furthermore, Christ "offered for all time a single sacrifice for sins . . . for by a single sacrifice he has perfected for all time those who are sanctified" (10:12-14).

4. God never sent Christ to the earth out of wrath, but only out of *love.* Most of us learned John 3:16 as children, but it seems we often forget what it says: "For God so loved the world that he gave his only Son, that whoever believes in him should not perish but have eternal life." No elements of hate, wrath, or punishment are present in the death of Christ. But we do find the elements of love, care, and atonement in great abundance.

When we see Jesus' death as God's redeeming love, we can respond to Christ with the same faith that was shared by the New Testament writers and the thousands of believers in the first century Church.

For some, however, who travel in the world's fast lanes of sophistication, or find themselves too insecure to respond to any stimuli except the latest "in" thing, reacting to Christ positively will always be a problem. Cardinal Jean-Marie Lustiger, the archbishop of Paris whose goals are for "spiritual conversion, not reform" in a country where the Church has all but died, understands the problem modern man is confronted with: "As things stand now, to say you believe Jesus is the son of God is going to become an enormous act of courage."[9]

To say that one believes in Jesus Christ, and that He is the divine Son of God is simply not the "in" thing to do in worldly crowds.

But God's redeeming love in Christ calls even the fearful to experience the abundance of His grace and power.

Whatever one thinks of Jesus today, whether they are as satisfied with Him as the first century Church was, or whether their faith has yet to rise to that level, one thing is clear: Jesus Christ *is* the Church.

It was Christ who founded the Church in God's will.

It was Christ who has given life and power to His Church down through the centuries of its history — to the very people who *are* His Church.

Jesus Christ is indissolubly linked to His Church as its very center, its breath of life.

Dietrich Bonhoeffer, who gave his life for Christ and His Church, being hanged by the Nazis in 1945 for his opposition to Hitler's atrocities, shares these insights on the unity of Christ and His Church:

> Jesus Christ is at once himself and his Church . . . To be in Christ therefore means to be in the Church. But if we are in the Church we are verily and bodily in Christ. The Church is the real presence of Christ . . . We should think of the Church not as an institution, but as a *person*, though of course a person in a unique sense.[10]

Jesus Christ never forsakes His Church because He cannot do so. He comes to us every day with wisdom, help, and strength if we are willing to reach out to Him in faith, no matter how feeble that effort might be. This was the secret of the apostle John, who was believed to be over ninety years old when he wrote these words concerning Christ and His Church:

> That which was from the beginning, which we have heard, which we have seen with our eyes, which we have

looked upon and touched with our hands concerning the word of life . . . we proclaim also to you, so that you may have fellowship with us; and our fellowship is with the Father and with his Son Jesus Christ (1 John 1:1-3).

Neither Jesus Christ nor the fellowship with God which is in Him can ever be limited to a special few. For Christ *is* His Church. And His Church is neither Catholic nor Protestant.

Rather, His Church is the people of a common faith, wherever He is found in the hearts of human beings the world over.

4

We Can Still Have the Faith of Mary and Paul

Life was slowly ebbing for the widow and her son, who lived on the shores of the Mediterranean Sea in the little Phoenician village of Zarepath (modern Sarafand, midway between two ancient Lebanese cities, Tyre and Sidon). In the mid-ninth century before Christ, drought and famine were ravaging the land.

History catches up to this courageous lady gathering sticks at the gate of the city. While twigs to build a fire may be plentiful, food is not. There is enough flour and oil for one more meal she and her son will share--but that is all. Thoughts of death prey heavily on her mind.

A man approaches—a hot and dusty man who is obviously very thirsty. A man who, no doubt, is also suffering from the drought and famine.

"Bring me a little water in a vessel, that I may

drink," he says. It is more of an order than a request. *How does he know,* she wonders, that she does have a little well water, enough, at least, for one who thirsts.

She drops her sticks and starts off for the water, silently asking God how long it will be before even the well runs dry. The man's voice stabs at her silent preoccupation with death. "Bring me a morsel of bread in your hand."

What? Bread? He wants bread? He must be a stranger passing through from the north—a foolish man who doesn't realize that he came the wrong way. She turns, staring sharply. *Ah, he's a Hebrew. Well, he won't get any bread from me.*

"As the Lord your God lives," she says, "I have nothing baked, only a handful of meal in a jar, and a little oil in a cruse. And now I'm gathering a couple of sticks, that I may go in and prepare it for myself and my son, that we may eat it, and die."

A slight smile appears on the man's tired but determined features. "Fear not. Go and do as you have said. But first make me a little cake of it and bring it to me, and afterward make for yourself and your son—"

Afterward? What sort of man is this who would say, *Feed me first. Then yourself—if there's anything left!*

"—for thus says the Lord the God of Israel, 'The jar of meal shall not be spent, and the cruse of oil shall not fail, until the day that the Lord sends rain upon the earth.'"

For a brief moment the Phoenician lady stared at this self-assured Hebrew. Surely he was a man of God, perhaps even a prophet. But why would he come to her with a promise of blessing from God? Her people were related to the Canaanites, whom the Hebrews had overrun and all but destroyed long ago. Hebrews still considered Phoenicians foreigners, although she knew that craftsmen from Tyre had helped Solomon build his great temple in Jerusalem many years ago.

Could God love her as He loved the Hebrews?

Faith in the Hebrew's words suddenly welled up in her heart like water gushing from a newborn spring. It had to be true! She and her son would not die! God would sustain them!

And it was true.

She and her son and the prophet Elijah ate for many days. The jar of flour did not run out. The cruse of oil did not run dry.

It was not according to their physical efforts that this was so, for drought and famine still raged throughout the land. Rather, they experienced this ancient miracle because the faith of their hearts rose up to meet the God of miracles (see 1 Kings 17:8-24 for the whole story).

Wherever God's people were in ancient times, are now in the present time, or will be in future generations of those yet born, faith exists. Wherever God is worshiped among Catholics and Protestants, a common faith exists and unites Christ's Church.

For God's people are a people of faith.

Yet faith is not a tangible entity. Neither is it a set of rules and regulations. It is not a creed recited in worship services, nor a list of beliefs printed in a Sunday church bulletin. And perhaps most important of all, at least for the modern person to come to grips with, faith is not subject to scientific scrutiny, for faith is neither scientific nor unscientific.

Faith is of the *heart.*

Faith is a human being's *response to God.*

Faith is *trust* in God.

All of these concepts of faith are what the writer of Hebrews talks about when he says, "Faith is the assurance of things hoped for, the conviction of things not seen. For by it the men of old received divine approval" (11:1-2).

He goes on to say that it is impossible to please God without faith. "For whoever would draw near to God must believe that he exists and that he rewards those who seek him" (11:6). Hebrews Chapter Eleven is a litany of Old Testament people, both men and women, who accomplished much—sometimes the extraordinary—through their faith in God.

Why can't Christians have a dynamic faith?— just like the saints of old.

The truth is that Christians of today *can* have this same kind of faith. For faith has never been the property of a chosen few. Anyone can have a dynamic faith in God — the "whoever" that Hebrews speaks of.

This is not to say that faith always comes easy. Moses, the greatest of all the ancient Hebrews, struggled with his faith. He believed in God, but when God asked him to go tell Egypt's ruling Pharaoh to free his Hebrew brothers and sisters from slavery, Moses bluntly told God, "I can't do that. Get somebody else."

But God showed Moses that he really did have faith. It lay hidden beneath his fears and insecurities, like the faith of many of us.

The Phoenician widow woman was different. Her faith was not instantaneous, but neither was it a struggle. Elijah asked her to do something a destitute person shouldn't be asked to do, and then, over her objections, told her that her actions would precipitate a miracle.

She believed him.

And there was a miracle!

God supplied her with food until the famine and drought were over.

Some Bible scholars and laity in the modern Church object to this story because it is unscientific. They believe it never happened as the Old Testament writers tell it. Food can't just "multiply." The whole story was designed to get the Hebrew people to worship the one true God instead of idols.

The objectors to these stories of biblical faith and miracles would have us believe that they must be relegated to the realm of religious superstition. People of modern science cannot honestly digest this nonsense. It is just this type of negative thinking—really a lack of belief in the God portrayed in the Bible—which hinders many people in the Church from developing a dynamic faith.

They will never convince me.

I have plenty of doubts—just like everyone else. This is not unusual for a minister. Most of the great figures in the Bible had doubts and fears. But in the end they trusted God.

And I've learned to trust God through my doubts and fears, even for answers to the little problems which so often vex us.

When I was a doctoral student at the Graduate Theological Union, the requirement of varying proficiencies in *six* languages presented a formidable problem. Nevertheless, I decided I could conquer this problem with God's help and my own diligence.

I passed exams in biblical Greek and Hebrew, but modern German presented a particular difficulty for me. I had no background in the language and failed the first exam. Wisdom prevailed and I obtained the services of a German tutor, a patient man by the name of Gerhard Schmitt. Despite his capable tutoring in his native language, I still wasn't sure I could pass the exam.

I studied hard and prayed hard, and the day soon came.

The exam was a portion of a work by the early nineteenth century philosopher, Georg Wilhelm Hegel. The piece was a commentary on the Bible, and some of the words were archaic. I prayed harder.

Following the exam many of the students who took it and failed complained about the way the German exams were administered. This led to the entire program being revamped.

But I passed with primary proficiency!

When I called Mr. Schmitt with the exciting news, he was amazed. Even he thought this particular exam had been unfair. Two of his superior students had failed, one of whom had walked out in disgust.

No one will ever convince me that God didn't help me pass that exam. I latched on to Hegel's thought pattern in the first paragraph, and from there on the whole passage seemed to flow in my mind. I guessed at some of the archaic spellings, translating with words that seemed to fit. I guessed right. Surely God was with me.

Did I cheat by asking—and getting—God's help? Not at all. I never asked God to give me the answers. I simply asked God to help me think better than I'd ever thought before. I needed a miracle and I received a miracle.

This is the same faith—the faith of one's heart—that enabled the widow lady to receive a miracle supply of flour and oil twenty-eight hundred years ago in ancient Palestine.

The basic problem with those who hold a negative view of biblical faith and the resulting miracles is that they fail either to understand or believe the real nature of God. Faith in God's existence demands belief in a being who transcends all that man is, all that nature is, and all that science is.

Genesis, the first book in the Bible, tells us that God is the creator of the universe. If this is true—and scientific evidence says that it is—then God Himself is the *creator of science.*

It is simply not a problem for God to intervene in the natural order of things and perform a pure and simple miracle.

Let the skeptics ridicule if they must. Skepticism about God and His power is not new. Although lack of faith in God is more rampant in our age because of a greater understanding of nature and the way things work, unbelief in the God of miracles has existed for quite some time.

Pharaoh, for example, laughed when Moses told him that God would destroy him if he didn't release the Hebrew slaves. After all, hadn't Egypt conquered many nations and built the great pyramids? What greater things could the god of slaves do?

But with God's miraculous intervention in the affairs of human beings, the Hebrews fled their captors—right out of Egypt and across a body of water that proved impossible for the pursuing Egyptians to cross.

People who don't believe the story of the widow woman and Elijah don't believe this story as the biblical historians tell it, either. But nobody has offered a better version of how a small band of defenseless slaves—men, women, and children—pulled off such an incredible feat.

The skeptics, whether ancient or modern, have never believed in the power of God. But for those who believe that He exists and that He rewards those who seek Him, the impossible is but a mountain to climb or a fear to conquer.

Perhaps in all of history nobody has been asked to believe anything more impossible than Mary, the mother of Jesus.

The Gospel writer, Luke, tells us that Mary was at first fearful and then incredulous when an angel of the Lord appeared to her and told her that she would conceive a child who would be called "the Son of the Most High." Mary was a simple Jewish maiden—a virgin who had entered into a legal contract (betrothal) to marry a man named Joseph. She was not a scientist nor a sophisticate, but neither was she ignorant of life.

"How can this be," she questioned, "since I do not know a man?"

The angel Gabriel responded:

> "The Holy Spirit will come upon you,
> and the power of the Most High will
> overshadow you; therefore the child to

be born will be called holy, the Son of God."

Although a visitation by an angel of the Lord is in itself miraculous, Gabriel sensed that Mary was still skeptical from having her senses so suddenly and unexpectedly jolted. He assured her that she need not be alarmed or uncertain about what she was seeing and hearing, for a similar miracle was already underway.

"Your kinswoman Elizabeth in her old age has also conceived a son. This is the sixth month with her who was called barren." Although Elizabeth was past bearing age and childless, she would soon give birth to the forerunner of Christ, John the Baptist. No virgin birth is hinted at here, for she had long been married to a priest of Israel named Zechariah. But conception for her was phenomenal.

The angel's explanation to Mary for the twin miracles was both transcendent and evocative: "With God nothing will be impossible."

As a human being Mary certainly had many doubts and fears. But she believed in God. She believed in His love and in His power. As she stood in the angel's presence, her faith surged within her. Excitedly, she boldly exclaimed, "I am the handmaid of the Lord! Let it be to me according to your word!" (See Luke 1:26-38 for the whole story).

Mary is not the only person of great faith that we

encounter in this miraculous story of Jesus' conception and birth. We must also consider Mary's fiancé, Joseph, who was shocked and deeply hurt when he discovered that Mary was pregnant. Joseph knew he was not the father and decided to end their engagement quietly.

But one night an angel of the Lord appeared to him also, this time in a dream. "Joseph son of David, do not be afraid to take Mary home as your wife, because what is conceived in her is from the Holy Spirit. She will give birth to a son, and you are to give him the name Jesus, because he will save his people from their sins" (Matt. 1:18-25, NIV).

Like Mary, Joseph believed in the God of love and miracles. Faith took control of his heart and mind. No longer was he ashamed to take Mary for his wife.

In analyzing this story of the virgin birth of Jesus, we might put ourselves in Joseph's and Mary's sandals and wonder if our doubts would turn to faith as easily as theirs did. For they certainly didn't believe such an incredible thing as a virgin birth was possible. What changed their minds wasn't merely the appearances of the angel. Rather, it was the declaration of the angel that such a birth could and would occur *by the power of the Holy Spirit.*

This was God's doing. And with God nothing is impossible.

Some Catholics and Protestants today scoff at belief in Christ's virgin birth. A Jewish myth, some say. Pagan ideas, others say. An early Christian invention to give more credence to the belief in Jesus' divinity, still others say.

If a person has little or no faith in God, or no faith in His ability to miraculously intervene in human affairs, the virgin birth is indeed impossible to believe. But before we label it just another myth of history, we need to realize a few things about this beautiful and wondrous story of faith and power and love.

First of all, attempts to relate the story to Jewish, pagan, or various religious cultures of the time of Christ are futile. No other culture has left a written record of any event closely approximating a virgin birth, not even in mythology.

In the history of the Church, the story is early. Some scholars have asserted that it was a later addition to Matthew and Luke to bolster faith in Christ against encroaching heresies. Evidence from the oldest Greek manuscripts of the New Testament, however, does not support this theory. Furthermore, the Church fathers of the second century referred to the virgin birth as a major Christian belief. Ignatius did so as early as A.D. 110. An early form of the Apostles' Creed, which dates back to the second century, contained the clause, "born of the Holy Spirit and the virgin Mary."[11]

The Gospels themselves, however, give us a solid clue as to the source of the story. Although the birth narratives in Matthew and Luke differ somewhat (Matthew gives us the story from

Joseph's point of view, while Luke tells it from Mary's), they are in harmony. Joseph Fitzmyer finds *twelve* common details in the two narratives, some of which are mentioned elsewhere in the New Testament even though the virgin birth is not.[12]

Inasmuch as each account contains personal details from the lives of Joseph and Mary, especially the latter, logic tells us that the original story could have been told *only by Mary herself.* It is not stated that Mary knew Matthew and Luke, but she did know the apostle John, who knew them both. In either case, Luke states that he was told the story of Jesus Christ by those who had known Him (Luke 1:2-4).

While a Jewish maiden and later a young mother, Mary never would have admitted the virgin birth to anyone. Had the story gone beyond believers in Christ, she likely would have been stoned for adultery.

But after Jesus had been put to death and resurrected by God to return to His rightful home in heaven, we find that Mary is one of the faithful believers who waits for the coming of the Holy Spirit in power on the Day of Pentecost (Acts 1:14).

By this time, Mary had no doubts that the baby Jesus, conceived in her womb by this same Holy Spirit, was indeed the Son of God and the Savior of the world. Now she could tell the Church. Those who had faith in God and faith that Jesus was the Christ would accept her story and share its wonder with others in the young Church.

Even those of us who believe this story must admit that all efforts to explain Jesus' virgin birth according to the knowledge of modern science end in failure. It is a matter of *faith.* It is faith in the God who has never been bound by the laws of nature known to mankind. It is faith in Jesus Christ as God's Son—the Savior who has never failed us nor forsaken us.

This is the faith of the widow woman in Elijah's day.

This is the faith of Mary in Jesus' day.

This is the faith that sustains us against life's struggles in our day.

This is the faith which believes that God is *not* unfathomable and unapproachable as both Catholic and Protestant fundamentalism have sometimes portrayed Him, or distant and powerless as liberalism would often have us believe.

It is a faith which believes that God loves us and is eager to help us and provide for us if we will acknowledge Him and seek His help.

This is not to say that God's love coupled with our faith always produces a happy ending—at least not always in this life. We need only look at Stephen, the Church's first martyr, to realize that the people of God have sometimes died because of their faith. This is the history of the Church.

But the whole point of the biblical stories of men and women of faith is that God *does* care for us deeply. And because He cares He does indeed intervene in our lives—if we allow Him to do so.

Jesus emphasized God's care repeatedly. "Look at the birds of the air," He said. "They neither sow nor reap nor gather into barns, and yet your heavenly Father feeds them. Are you not of more value than they? . . . Consider the lilies of the field, how they grow. They neither toil nor spin . . . If God so clothes the grass of the field, which today is alive and tomorrow is thrown into the oven, will he not much more clothe you? . . . But seek first his kingdom and his righteousness, and all these things shall be yours as well" (Matt. 6:25-34).

Here is faith—trust in a living, loving God. Trusting God precipitates experiencing God. Jesus did not mean, of course, that we could sit and wait for all the blessings of heaven to fall into our laps. I've known people who tried this. One young man told me, "I can't see myself getting a job in the near future. It interferes with my Bible study." I never did find out how much Bible studying he actually did, but lack of a job definitely interfered with paying his bills.

What Jesus meant was that as we go about life's business, our hearts should be centered in serving God. When we have this kind of desire, our faith in God will help us through life's toughest moments.

This is exactly the place at which many skeptics within and without the Church head down a rubble-strewn path. They think that trusting

Christians have a blind faith, a faith that says "I believe" only because mother believed or because a preacher scared them into believing. Some do have this kind of "belief." But this is not faith.

Real faith is an intangible expression of the heart and the spirit, the very being of mankind. Faith is a knowing, a certainty even in the midst of doubts, that God exists and that He rewards those who seek Him.

Faith cannot bypass our intellect, yet it must, at times, as with the case of the Phoenician widow, supersede our intellect. Food cannot multiply by itself. That's in opposition to the laws of nature. But God created flour and oil! It's not a problem for Him to multiply food. But intellect cannot tell us this. Faith tells us this. And it is faith that experiences the power of God.

This was how the apostle Paul came to live his life following his acceptance of Jesus as his Savior and Lord. As he wrote to the Galatians, "The life I now live in the flesh I live by faith in the Son of God" (2:20).

Paul is not speaking here of some mystical or ethereal union with God. Nor is he speaking of faith as simply believing correct doctrines. Rather, Paul is talking about a life-changing and life-giving faith that sustained him in life's difficulties, a faith that would one day place him in God's eternal presence.

This is faith, first of all, in Jesus Christ, who gives salvation to all who come to Him. And it is a lifelong experience of faith in the living God. It is not a blind faith because it is a faith of the heart, a faith which in a very real sense knows and experiences the God who created us.

Yet in another sense one might say that faith is indeed "blind" because it cannot actually see or prove beyond a doubt that God exists. "Faith is the assurance of things hoped for, the conviction of things not seen." But even as the writer of Hebrews penned these words with unshakable faith, he could offer no scientific proof that God existed.

Neither could Paul. He was forced to say, "We walk by faith, not by sight" (2 Cor. 5:7). Paul could not prove God's existence to someone else. Yet he had proved God's existence for himself because he had experienced God through his faith.

Although suffering many hardships and once left for dead after being stoned, Paul traveled all over the Mediterranean preaching Christ and establishing churches of new believers. As he did so, he worked many miracles through the power of the Holy Spirit. Paul did not need to capture God in a bottle and dissect Him in order to verify His existence.

God was working in Paul's life through his own personal faith. His belief in God was a knowing deep within his soul that neither hardship nor persecution could erase.

Paul never forgot any of his experiences of God.

And it was Paul's day to day experience of God and of the Christ he loved that also gave him a great faith in the hope of a future life. He writes, "Indeed I count everything as loss because of the surpassing worth of knowing Christ Jesus my Lord. For his sake I have suffered the loss of all things . . . that I may know him and the power of his resurrection, and may share his sufferings, becoming like him in his death, that if possible I may attain the resurrection from the dead" (Phil. 3:8-11).

Paul preached Christ to the known world not because he had to, but because he wanted men and women everywhere to share his faith in Christ and in the hope of a better life in this world and in a future, perfect life forever in God's presence.

Paul believed in a future resurrection of the dead even before he gave his life to Christ. He was a Pharisee, and the Pharisees believed in the resurrection at the end of time.

But with Jesus something new and different had happened. God had raised Him up from the grave shortly after His death. Jesus had once again walked in the land of Palestine. Paul believed this because, as he tells us in 1 Corinthians, Jesus not only appeared to Peter and more than five hundred of His followers, but "he appeared also to me" (15:4-8).

Paul might have rationalized this appearance of Jesus on the road to Damascus by telling himself, "Well, maybe I dreamed the whole thing. It's pretty wild to believe that this man Jesus was raised from the grave as His followers have been claiming."

Surely Paul had doubts at first. After all, he had

blasphemed Christ and persecuted His followers. But as God ministered to him through the faith of others, especially through Ananias, Paul realized that his new experiences of Jesus were real. As his faith grew in God's love and forgiveness, it also grew in the resurrected Christ and in the future hope of the resurrection of all believers.

Some Catholics and Protestants today don't believe the resurrection stories of Jesus in the Gospels, nor in any hope of a future resurrection. The dead don't *really* rise up again—who's ever proved anything so absurd? That's just a symbol of new life and hope in the Christian community. Modern people can't be expected to believe that nonsense any more than they can be expected to believe in any miracle. Our hope is in this life, not any non-existent after-life.

This is what some in the Church are saying today. Not only have they abandoned the God of miracles, but they have abandoned the God who promises mankind eternal life beyond this earth-bound existence through His Son, Jesus Christ.

At issue is not simply one of the scientific mind versus the medieval mind, as many would lead us to believe. Although the people in Paul's day didn't have computers, turbo-powered automobiles, and lasers, their reflections on life often gave rise to scientific and philosophic observations.

They also lacked accumulative knowledge, yet we still marvel at many of the engineering and metallurgical feats of the Egyptians, Greeks, and Romans, as well as later civilizations such as those built by the Mayas, Aztecs, and unknown people in the Americas.

Thus, even the people in Jesus' day were faced with a difficulty in believing that a dead man could rise from the grave. When Paul preached the resurrection of Christ to Greeks at the Areopagus, the open forum for philosophers in Athens, "some mocked. But others said, 'We will hear you again about this'" (Acts 17:32). Their understanding of history, coupled with empirical observations, told them that this kind of thing didn't happen.

Science today has studied inconclusively (some believe; some scoff—it's the same old story) the accounts of people who have been medically dead for a few moments and who tell of seeing their deceased loved ones or a place of light and beauty. Others, on their death beds, have been known to smile and talk to angels or to departed family members immediately before passing from this life.

Several years ago my wife experienced the tragedy of the death of two cousins only months apart. Richard, a male nurse, was killed when an ambulance in which he was riding collided with another vehicle and exploded. Alfred, a mechanic, died from an infection he contracted following an operation.

Not long before Alfred passed away, he suddenly mentioned seeing a bright light. Then he said, "Hello, Grandma . . . Oh! Richard!" His godly grandmother had died a few years earlier. And Richard, a person so loved by the hospital staff where he worked that they dedicated a garden to his memory, was his cousin who had recently died.

Yet Alfred talked to them as though they were at his bedside.

Does this experience—and many like them—prove that there is such a place as heaven and a future resurrection? No. What people see and experience is known only to them. The skeptics readily explain all such phenomena as "psychologically or medically induced."

However, such experiences do provide encouragement to those who believe God's promise of eternal life. No one—not a scientist or a theologian—can prove or disprove the existence of heaven and life beyond the grave.

Paul believed it and promised us the same because he, through following Christ, had come to experience the reality of God in a new dimension. He defused the skeptics of his day—many of whom were Greeks in the churches he had established—by stating, "If for this life only we have hoped in Christ, we are of all men most to be pitied. But in fact Christ has been raised from the dead, the first fruits of those who have fallen asleep" (1 Cor. 15:19-20).

No one—try though they did—could convince Paul that Christ was a fraud and eternal life was merely an empty promise of pie-in-the-sky.

Paul trusted in God. And he said in 1 Corinthians 15 that more than 500 people including the apostles — and himself — had seen the risen Christ.

What of us today? Not even painstaking Bible scholars and Church historians who believe in the resurrection can provide us with absolute proof that Jesus rose from the grave. But Thomas Bokenkotter, who is both theologian and historian in the Catholic church, does make an important observation concerning the stories of the empty tomb in the Gospels: A strong argument supporting the empty tomb is the fact that it was discovered by *women.* The same story, with some variations, is told in all four Gospels.

In Jesus' day, women could not be used as witnesses according to Jewish law. A story of Jewish origin using women as witnesses — even though they were women of faith in Christ — would not likely have been invented.[13]

Yet neither Bokenkotter nor other theologians can say conclusively that Jesus rose from the grave. The hope of a future resurrection to eternal life is a matter of *faith*, but it is our faith which gives us a *certainty* of a future resurrection to life forever with our great God.

Because when we, with Paul and Christians of all ages, overcome temptations, hardships, afflictions, and all sorts of adversities because of our faith in a loving God, we are assured that His promise of eternal life is not a fraud. No wonder the apostle John said with a bold certainty:

> Whatever is born of God overcomes the world; and this is the victory that overcomes the world, our faith. Who is it that overcomes the world but he who believes that Jesus is the Son of God? (1 John 5:4-5).

The real Church is a Church of faith in the living Christ. As God's people, Christians everywhere walk by faith, not by sight, upheld and energized by the power of Christ and the Holy Spirit.

Because of their faith, God's people know and experience the living God and know that His promises are true.

On his second visit to the United States in 1987, Pope John Paul II aptly stated this very point in a speech to thousands of Catholic youth:

> "Without faith in God, there can be no hope, no lasting authentic hope. To stop believing in God is to start down a path that can lead only to emptiness and despair. But those who have the gift of faith live with confidence about things to come. They look to the future with anticipation and joy, even in the face of suffering and pain; and the future that

they are ultimately looking toward is everlasting life with the Lord."

This is the kind of faith that experiences God in the midst of the harsh realities of life, a faith that is not peculiar to a chosen few, but a faith that can enrich the life of anyone who chooses to have it.

This is the faith of Mary and Paul and anyone who dares to believe.

This is the kind of faith which both creates and demonstrates the common bond Catholics and all Protestants have in and through our risen Savior, Jesus Christ.

5

Fellowship Through Christ's Spiritual Calling

For me there is no greater thrill than sharing the gospel with another human being. It doesn't seem to matter whether I'm communicating from the pulpit, writing, or just chatting about Jesus Christ and the Christian life.

I simply love being a Christian and being a minister.

Yet I must confess I sometimes find myself a little bit embarrassed to be known as a Christian and a minister.

Too many Christians and too many ministers display so little of Christ and the spirituality He has called us to that the world often cannot resist the

99

temptation to throw all Christians and ministers—especially ministers—into a trash can marked PHONIES.

This is especially true in the Catholic Church now that so much sexual abuse by priests has come to light. People outside the Catholic Church choose to believe that the *entire* church harbors sexual predators. Faithful Catholics know that this is not true. In fact, less than 4% of priests have been identified as sexually abusive. Even .001% is too many, for there should be *no* sexual predators in Christ's Church.

Sadly, as I pointed out in the Preface, even Protestants and contemporary evangelical churches have their faithless, sexual deviates who, though they claim to be ministers, are devoid of the presence and power of Jesus Christ.

A few years ago I was surprised to hear that a fairly well-known Pentecostal minister had divorced his wife and married a much younger woman. He certainly was not the first minister to do that, but Pentecostals preached long and loud against the evils of divorce. At the time I was working for a Christian organization, and a fellow worker and I got into a conversation about the divorce.

"That's a sad situation," he said, shaking his head. "I used to work for the man. He was having an affair with the younger woman for some time before he got a divorce. I tried to talk to him about it, but he insisted that what the Bible says about adultery didn't apply to him."

I've been hearing about adultery in the Church ever since I was a boy and my father told me about a missionary who'd been called home for running around with another man's wife. The only story of adultery that really shocked me was when one of my good Christian friends "fell in love" with his secretary and, after a short affair, divorced his wife for her. No one could talk him out of it. Several years later he realized his mistake.

God does indeed forgive us for our sins when we're truly repentant. The sin of adultery is no exception.

But there's always a hurt and a deep disappointment when a Christian leader fails miserably in his calling, when he or she will not do the very things they teach others.

Why not? Isn't the Christ they preach and teach residing within them? Isn't God's Holy Spirit more powerful than the passions of the flesh and more persuasive than the frailties of our own thoughts?

This is the ideal, but it is not always the reality of any given person's Christian life. Christ will not reside in our lives any more than we let Him. Neither will the Holy Spirit guide and empower us if we don't want Him to.

All too often, it seems, the tugs of purely human passions and desires pull us away from the gentle persuasion of Christ's calling to spirituality.

To turn away from Christ's calling to live a holy and righteous life may not only mean shipwreck in our own lives, but it also has a profound affect on the Church as a whole.

For the spirituality of Christ and the disciples, a life mindful of and dedicated to the things of the Holy Spirit as opposed to earthly and sensual matters, is the meeting ground of a common faith. Catholics and Protestants can share that faith not only because we believe in Christ, but because He has called us to the same spirituality.

And where that life is lived there is a natural, shared faith, a drawing together of those who live in a certain manner because their Savior has called them to that life.

Yet many Christians today—even priests and ministers—seem to find spirituality a hard life to live.

Why don't Christians display more spirituality?

My search for the answer to the problem started a couple of years before God called me into the ministry.

It was the early 60s and I'd just enlisted in the Army Reserve. While waiting for boot camp to begin, I took a temporary job at a tiny factory near my home in Southern California. I'd worked only a few hours when the owner called me into his office.

"You have a different look in your eyes than a lot of people," he said. "Are you a Christian by any chance?"

"Well, yes, I am."

"What church?" I'm sure he couldn't resist asking that question.

"The Christian Church."

He thought a moment. "That's good. I'm a Baptist myself. Sure is nice to hire a man who thinks like I do."

For the moment I thought so too. But I soon realized I didn't think all that much like him.

The worker he assigned to be my instructor was a Mexican who spoke little English. He was friendly, and it took me only a day to realize that he not only knew his job but that he also worked hard. The third day I was there he came to me with tears in his eyes. He pulled out his paycheck stub.

"Look," he sputtered. "I make so little. I can hardly buy food for my family."

I couldn't believe the numbers on his stub. He was making only half what I was getting, and I was only temporary.

"Please," he begged. "Talk to the boss for me. I work so hard."

I promised him I would. 1 didn't see the problem since the boss was a Christian. Maybe he didn't understand the man's situation.

I talked to the boss, but he only got angry.

"I'm not paying him a penny more!" he shouted, slamming his fist on the desk. "He's a Mexican, in case you haven't noticed. They're all a bunch of lazy, no-goods."

Perhaps I hadn't really thought about it before, but this was the first time I can recall realizing how some people talked and acted like Christians on Sundays, but failed to always be Christians the rest of the week.

When I left for boot camp I still felt sorry for my fellow laborer, but I never figured out how to help him. In those days I didn't know that many employers, Christian or otherwise, systematically exploited undocumented workers.

Some Christians prefer to excuse unchristian behavior with the well-worn cliché, "Well, we're all human." This excuse is acceptable when we slip and fail God. But this excuse will never work for Christians whose sins have become permanent attitudes of the heart.

Other Christians would complain that I'm just picking on Pentecostals and Baptists because I don't like them, or because I think my church is better than theirs.

This is, after all, the charade many Christians like to play. We become convinced that *our* church is the only church which truly understands and lives to the fullest God's pure way, especially when it comes to spirituality. Everyone else, somehow, has gotten off the track.

This is the history of the Church from the second century to the present, especially since the Reformation. Catholics and Protestants have flung an endless stream of accusations against each other from the day Martin Luther posted his *95 Theses* on the door of the Castle Church in Wittenberg, Germany, in 1517.

Protestants began warring against each other not long after the ink on Luther's *Theses* was dry, not only over the matter of spirituality, but over theology and practices as well. To the discredit of the Church and the sorrow of God's heart, the wars continue today.

We find it difficult not to yield to the temptation of condemning other churches simply because we know one bad apple in the lot, or, worse yet, accept a false accusation made by an over-zealous Christian.

And while we're condemning others we ignore or excuse the sins in our own church.

The truth is that while we may prefer our own church for personal reasons, God doesn't see any particular entity in the body of Christ as superior to another. *People are people.* None of us are perfect. Neither are we totally depraved. Rather, both Catholics and Protestants are somewhere between these two extremes.

All of us are people for whom Christ died. And all of us are people with whom God is striving to make us more like Christ.

As a Protestant minister, it's always a joy to meet and associate with Catholics who love and serve Jesus Christ just as much as any Protestant I know. I've had this exhilarating experience with priests, nuns, and the laity alike.

I get the same feeling of joy from sharing with spiritual people in Protestant denominations other than my own. I have good friends, for instance, in Pentecostal churches whom I admire and respect because of their love for Christ, their love for others, and their abiding spirituality.

I know fewer Baptists, who have often been staunch critics of Pentecostals (and Catholics, too), but I respect them. My ancestor, Thomas Angell, was a founding member of the first Baptist church in America. He came here with the founder of the Baptist church, Roger Williams, in 1631, and was deeded a large piece of land when Williams laid out the town of Providence, Rhode Island. A portion of Thomas Angell's original lot is now a part of the First Baptist Church property in Providence.

Although I have never been a member of a Baptist church, I hold a special place for them in my heart. They are today a great evangelizing force for Christ in America and around the world as well.

Saints abound in every church. Unfortunately, it is more often the stories of unspiritual people which are passed from church to church and which sometimes make the public media. We need look no further than both Catholics and Southern Baptists, slammed and condemned, rightfully so, for sexual abuses. Yet all the good faithful and Christ-loving people have done over the years in both churches is often overlooked.

It is, tragically, the negative stories which often

have a greater impact on the non-Christian world. Yet it is also true that many good Christians have stopped attending church because a priest or a minister or a lay person proved to be something other than the Christian he or she professed to be.

Why don't Christians display more spirituality?

I've observed two basic reasons:

1. Some people honestly don't know what spirituality is.

2. Others just don't have a desire to attain the level of spirituality God intends for His people. Included in the latter category are those who erroneously but sometimes sincerely substitute their own ideas of spirituality for God's.

In the first category there is a very large segment of Christians who confuse spirituality with mental assent or verbal agreement. They think that if they believe the right doctrines and say "yes" to everything their church stands for, they automatically become spiritual persons. This is a common notion of the essence of Christianity.

Furthermore, there is a prevalent misconception among people from many churches that external religious acts and appearances are inherently spiritual. The more often one attends church or Bible study, the more charitable deeds one does, or, perhaps, the more one gives in the offering plate, the more it is thought that one is indeed a very spiritual person.

Not necessarily. True spirituality is a matter of the heart.

Mental assent and external acts are never in and of themselves spiritual, for spirituality has to do with the *attitudes* of one's heart.

Others who profess Christianity seem to think that if they invoke the name of God or Christ often enough and engage in a lot of religious talk, it doesn't matter if at the same time they live in a manner alien to the holiness of God. A few priests and ministers have become particularly good at this. But professional reciting of prayers, liturgy, and sermons will never excuse ungodly living.

This is not to say that unholy living is always intentional. Sometimes Christians, even priests and ministers, are ignorant of God's ways because they have not adequately understood New Testament Christianity.

The failure to understand and practice true spirituality by those who appear or profess to be religious is not new. The Jews of Jesus' day had the same problem.

Although the religious community Jesus was bom into had produced a great number of spiritual people who truly served God with their lives, Jesus nevertheless encountered many religious people who didn't know God at all. The Gospel of Matthew records a long discourse of Jesus against the lack of spirituality in the lives of many Pharisees. A portion of it reads like a discourse against the Church of both the past and the present:

"Woe to you, scribes and Pharisees, hypocrites! for you tithe mint and dill and cumin, and have neglected the weightier matters of the law, justice and mercy and faith; these you ought to have done, without neglecting the others. You blind guides, straining out a gnat and swallowing a camel! (23:23-24).
"Woe to you, scribes and Pharisees, hypocrites! for you are like whitewashed tombs, which outwardly appear beautiful, but within they are full of dead men's bones and all uncleanness. So you also outwardly appear righteous to men, but within you are full of hypocrisy and iniquity" (23:27-28).

True spirituality is a matter of the heart.

Jesus tried to implant this concept of spirituality in His followers, not only through the love and compassion He demonstrated toward all who came to Him with physical, emotional, or spiritual needs, but also through teaching.

We see this especially in Jesus' commendation of a Jewish scribe (a Pharisee) who did understand the concept (Mark 12: 28-34). When the scribe asked which commandment was the greatest, Jesus responded from Deuteronomy 6: "The Lord our God, the Lord is one; and you shall love the Lord your God with all your heart, and with all your soul, and with all your mind, and with all your strength."

Evidently wanting the scribe to be certain that another commandment went hand-in-hand with the first, Jesus continued, this time from Leviticus 19: "The second is this, 'You shall love your neighbor as yourself.' There is no other commandment greater than these."

In all the bulk of Old Testament writings, Jesus offered two positive commandments, rather than the numerous "thou shalt nots," as the essence of true spirituality.

The scribe was happy with Jesus' answers. He responded, "You are right, Teacher. You have truly said that he is one, and there is no other but he; and to love him with all the heart, and with all the understanding, and with all the strength, and to love one's neighbor as oneself is much more than all whole burnt offerings and sacrifices."

Now Jesus affirmed the scribe's wise answer. "You are not far from the kingdom of God."

This scribe understood what the Baptist businessman I worked for did not. Attending church and believing the right doctrines does not make one a spiritual person. Rather, it is a heart that is right toward God and toward one's fellow human beings — *and that alone* — which makes one the spiritual person that Christ has called us to be.

When we truly follow Christ by yielding our lives to God and by loving others, sin cannot have a place in our lives. Yet how often do we see some of the sins Jesus warned us about in the lives of Christians today? He said:

> "What comes out of a man is what defiles a man. For from within, out of the heart of man, come evil thoughts, fornication, theft, murder, adultery, coveting, wickedness, deceit, licentiousness, envy, slander, pride, foolishness. All these evil things come from within, and they defile a man" (Mark 7:20-23).

The scribe who questioned Jesus already knew the difference between yielding to human passions and serving the living God. He had only to do one thing: yield his life to the Christ who had come in the flesh in the person of Jesus of Galilee.

Why don't we do this? Why don't we let the Christ we profess as Savior come fully into our lives so we can have the power of the Holy Spirit to live a truly spiritual life?

One major reason we don't is because we as human beings sometimes find it easier to follow the teachings of others rather than seek after God and His desire for our lives with our own hearts, our own minds, and our own strengths.

As pointed out in Chapter Two, *too many Christians simply don't think for themselves.*

This situation has always yielded enormous problems in Christian living, because the theology and direction of another human being may not be the theology and direction of God. In fact, it all too often is not. And then Jesus' observation of religious life in His day becomes a prophecy fulfilled in our day: "If a blind man leads a blind man, both will fall into a pit" (Matt. 15:14).

We get into the habit of letting others spoon-feed their brand of Christianity to us by seldom studying the Bible in the quietness of our own time, and by failing to meditate upon God's Word and seek His will through prayer. How much easier it is to let others do this for us.

But this is not God's way. God is not some impersonal, communal spirit, but a personal, loving Father who cares for us deeply and who ministers to each of us individually. Another Christian may introduce us to God through His Son, but to come to really know God and love Him in a personal way and to truly follow Christ in His calling for our lives is something we can do *only by ourselves.*

While I was working as a writer and editor for the Full Gospel Business Men's Fellowship International, I was often asked to answer letters from people with serious problems. One lady wrote that she was following the teachings of a certain charismatic teacher, who boldly proclaimed that if a person were really living the Christian life, he or she would get rich. The key to this was to give, give, give, in order to receive these financial riches from God.

This lady had given over and above her means, but she was only getting further into financial quicksand. What, she wanted to know, had happened to the riches "God" had promised her?

Her letter did not have an angry tone, but she was very discouraged and growing more bitter in her situation. I got the distinct impression that she did not blame the teacher, but thought that God was simply not keeping His promise. Furthermore, it appeared that she was totally absorbed with this "spiritual" quest.

I informed her that the particular teacher was in error. God has never promised riches as a reward for serving Christ. Jesus and the New Testament writers did promise us that if we sought God and His will, He would always supply our needs. Some Christians do become wealthy, just as a few saintly people in the Bible were wealthy. But this is not a general promise of God to the Church.

I encouraged the lady to study the Scriptures for herself rather than letting someone else formulate her understanding of the Christian life.

Blindly following churches, teachers, priests, ministers, and even lay preachers who promote error (it doesn't matter if this is done knowingly or unknowingly—the negative results are always the same) has been a problem for Christians throughout the history of the Church.

The problem has become rampant today with so many self-proclaimed teachers and Bible exegetes on the fundamentalist side of the Church, and the faithless who boldly confess to believing nothing on the other extreme of liberalism.

But the problem is an old one. In every generation there have been those within the Church who simply didn't understand the spiritual nature of the kingdom of God, or who really didn't care about the teaching of Jesus that spirituality begins by loving God with one's heart and mind and strength.

Many of those who didn't understand Jesus and the writers of the New Testament, or who chose to ignore them, have been leaders in the Church. And leaders beget sincere and honest followers even when they err. Followers, in turn, pass the errors from generation to generation.

The drift from the Church's understanding of true spirituality was slow, and although a general drift probably began in the late first century, the seeds began to germinate with vigor in the second century when some Church fathers began to emphasize works and laws. Once this had occurred, many Christians moved away from an internal experience of Christ to the externalizing of Christianity.

Fasting on certain days, praying certain prayers a specified number of times, and assent to certain doctrines soon became the norm by which people were identified with the Church and practiced their Christianity.

Those who knew that external religion alone was not the spirituality God looks for, whether clergy or laity, have always worshiped God from their hearts and showed that same love to their neighbors. We seem to read less of these saints, both Catholic and Protestant, than those who have erred throughout history, although they have existed in great numbers. Why else has the Church survived?

These are the Christians who have understood not only those two positive commandments of love toward God and neighbor, but also the words of faith and truth which Jesus shared with the Samaritan woman at Jacob's well long ago:

> "The hour is coming, and now is, when the true worshipers will worship the Father in spirit and truth, for such the Father seeks to worship him. God is spirit, and those who worship him must worship in spirit and truth" (John 4:23-24).

For some people, however, human passions and desires have drowned out the deeper longing of the soul for true spirituality and led to heartache and frustration.

Numerous examples of error duping those who

blindly trusted could be cited from Church history. One example in particular, however, stands out inasmuch as it contributed, in part, to the Reformation. Furthermore, the motivation for the error is alive and well today, especially among Protestants.

This is the problem of *money*. Everywhere I go, it seems, both Church members and non-church members are highly agitated over the Church's problem with money.

Yet the Church has always honestly needed money. Existing in a physical world, it cannot escape this need, As long as the Church receives tithes, free-will offerings, and pledges with no coercion, no exploitation, no exaction, and no manipulation, money is not a problem. Giving to God's work is spiritually rewarding.

But at various times and in various places, the Church of history has invented psychological means of extracting money from sincere followers of Jesus Christ, methods which have not only been fraudulent and greedy, but which have given a black name to Christianity by insulting Christ and turning God into an extortionist.

One of the methods some authorities in the medieval Catholic Church discovered and used lustily at times was the selling of *indulgences.* Originally, an indulgence was the remission of a temporal punishment for forgiven sin. But in the Middle Ages indulgences were being *sold* by professional salesmen either for the remission of one's own punishment, or of a departed loved one's time spent in purgatory.

Church historian Roland Bainton comments on the practice: "At first indulgences were conferred on those who sacrificed or risked their lives in fighting against the infidel, and then were extended to those who, unable to go to the Holy Land, made contributions to the enterprise. The device proved so lucrative that it was speedily extended to cover the construction of churches, monasteries, and hospitals. The gothic cathedrals were financed in this way."[14]

There is nothing inherently wrong with fundraising. But in Martin Luther's time fundraising through the sale of indulgences was nothing more than a fraudulent method of raising money.

This would not have happened except that most of the common folks could not read, or, if they could, did not have a Bible to read for themselves. Therefore, many people believed the claim that the only way to free themselves and their poor, wretched loved ones from a possible eternity in purgatory was to pay, pay, and pay the rapidly accelerating fees.

This scandalous activity was not the practice of the entire Catholic Church. But it was especially rampant in Germany where the chief hawker of indulgences, John Tetzel, made many fantastic claims concerning the little pieces of paper he sold.

He is the reputed author of the ditty:

"When the coin in the coffer rings, the soul from purgatory springs!"

If you really believed that God demanded you pay the Church—even your last coin—to release your departed family members from the torment of their punishment, wouldn't you pay to transfer them instantly to the eternal bliss of heaven?

Martin Luther was outraged. The mercy of God being peddled for money blasphemed His holiness and robbed the commoners of their means of existence. Complaints of extortion had been raised for years. But Luther, a simple monk, was the first person with the courage to successfully challenge the Church on the selling of indulgences.

Actually, Luther's ire was directed more toward the sellers of indulgences than Pope Leo X, whom he thought would be shocked by the claims of the sellers. The pope did reform some of the abuses in indulgences, and in 1567 these activities were prohibited by Pope Pius V.

Nevertheless, the unspiritual conduct by those who claimed to represent Christ and the Church had provided the springboard for the Reformation. Money was by no means the only issue of Luther's effort at reform, but its blatant misuse changed the course of the Church and the world as well.

The problem of money did not disappear with

the Reformation. It's still a problem today, especially among Protestants. The most notorious example is that of televangelists, who have concocted deceitful and manipulative ways to coerce their followers into donating. Sometimes incredibly large amounts of money have changed hands. But I also know of more than one local parish which lied to its members to get them to give to building funds.

In God's way of thinking, however, the end never justifies unspiritual means. God never approves of unchristian methods to achieve Christian purposes. (Not all church fundraising has been for God-ordained purposes. Giver beware!) Neither does God bully or scare people into giving.

Paul wrote the following advice to the Corinthian church, from whom he wished to receive an offering for the Christians in Judea who were suffering because of a famine:

> Each one must do as he has made up his mind, not reluctantly or under compulsion, for God loves a cheerful giver (2 Cor. 9:7).

Cheerful giving is true spirituality. Coercive giving is not.

As Christians of a long and sometimes dubious past, as Christians who come to the making of a new beginning each day the sun rises, each of us needs to make the determination to seek God on our own. This may not be easy to do if the theologies of our past have entrenched erroneous presuppositions in our minds and spirits.

But if we determine to seek God for ourselves, study the Bible with diligence, and follow Christ from the depths of our hearts, God's Holy Spirit will help us do just that.

The second basic reason why Christians don't display more spirituality is that some *just don't want to.* These people fall into two categories, the sincere and the not-so-sincere.

The latter group is easy to identify, but not so easy to motivate. Like a person with a mathematical mind who is satisfied to sweep factory floors, these people could be spiritual servants of Christ if they wanted to. They prefer to do next to nothing for Christ and often serve only their own appetites. They hang on, I suppose, dabbling in church life in the hope that they will at least squeak into heaven by the barest of margins.

This, at least, is what one of these Christians told me when I tried to motivate him. "I'm not too interested in spiritual things," he said. "If I can just make it to heaven I'll be happy."

All we can do for church members of this type is let them see that the Christian life really is exciting—not always perfect or what we dream or hope for, but exciting. It's exciting because God is a good God who loves us and helps us become what we ought to be and can be.

Why wouldn't a Christian (or a non-Christian for that matter) want this type of life? The hang-up, of course, is that some degree of spirituality is always associated with it.

But I'm encouraged for those who, often by their own confessions, don't want a high level of spirituality. The last time I saw the man who wasn't "too interested" in that higher level, he thanked me for teaching him about faith.

The other category of people who don't want to display more spirituality is often difficult to identify because these usually insist that they *are* more spiritual than other Christians. These are those who erroneously but sincerely substitute their own ideas of spirituality for God's.

This is an ancient problem, dating back to the beginning of human existence. It resulted not only in world-wide idolatry, but the brutal practice of human sacrifice, a form of worship quite prevalent in ancient societies and even practiced in a few dark and hidden communities today.

The problem of substituting human ideas of spirituality for God's ideas was summed up well by the apostle Paul in the context of Christian faith:

> The time is coming when people will not endure sound teaching, but having itching ears they will accumulate for themselves teachers to suit their own likings, and will turn away from listening

to the truth and wander into myths. (2 Timothy 4:3-4).

Here is the basis for many forms of *pseudo* spirituality.

Whereas *true* spirituality begins with a desire to be a servant of God and a servant of humanity, pseudo spirituality begins with a desire to accept God's ways only when it serves us.

People who desire a Christianity that suits them, rather than the Christianity Jesus initiated, do so because *they want God to be subject to them.*

Many sincere Christians have these attitudes without realizing it. They're always running after some new, "deep" teaching. Unable to yield themselves totally to Christ on His terms, they seek those teachings which seem to agree with what they would prefer God and Christianity to be like.

Those who want to be spiritual but don't like what Jesus and the New Testament writers had to say either ignore them, discount their testimony, or rework their words to suit their own ideas of what the Christian faith should be. Fundamentalists do this just as much as liberals do.

But this is nothing new. The same thing was happening in Paul's day. In a letter previous to Paul's "itching ears" warning to Timothy, he was already cautioning about teachers who did not agree "with the sound words of our Lord Jesus Christ and the teaching which accords with godliness" (1 Tim. 6:3).

The situation that occasioned Paul's warning in his first letter to Timothy occurred because some people decided to make God subject to themselves. They were teaching that godliness was a means of personal gain. Paul warned them:

> Those who desire to be rich fall into temptation, into a snare, into many senseless and hurtful desires that plunge men into ruin and destruction. For the love of money is the root of all evils; it is through this craving that some have wandered away from the faith and pierced their hearts with many pangs. But as for you, man of God, shun all this; aim at righteousness, godliness, faith, love, steadfastness, gentleness (1 Tim. 6:9-11).

Even in Paul's day some were turning the pursuit of godliness, or spirituality, into the pursuit of money.

Times don't seem to change. Even today many Christians are leaving the spiritual road of servanthood and sacrifice that Jesus Christ and His disciples paved to wander off onto the heavily-rutted dirt road of materialism. They believe the false premise of the deceptive *prosperity gospel* that it is their right as Christians to be wealthy.

Don't those who teach these things ever read these words of Paul? Don't they also read the words of Jesus and know that spirituality—love, faith, righteousness, godliness, and all that these things encompass—are at odds with the craving to be successful as the world views success?

Probably they do read these things. But Warren Wiersbe points out what it is that blinds people to the truth:

> The pop gospel of success tries to make us believe that God's greatest concern is to make us happy, not to make us holy, and that He is more concerned about the physical and the material than He is the moral and the spiritual. The "success god" is a celestial errand boy whose only responsibility is to respond to our every call and make sure that we are enjoying life.[15]

The "success god" is a god who is subject to human beings, but in reality this god is a fairy tale. For he is not the God of the Bible.

The God of the Bible does want us to be happy, to be sure. But He wants us to experience *true* happiness. That can only be achieved when we experience true spirituality. And true spirituality can be experienced only on God's terms, not ours.

The "success god," the god of materialism, will never bring any Christian that sense of inner peace and satisfaction. It may instead lead to inner turmoil and destruction.

But the pursuit of godliness, that true spirituality which begins by loving God and loving our neighbor, brings to our very beings a sense of joy and peace and harmony that not even the world's troubles can vanquish.

The "godly" pursuit of money is not the only myth that Christians substitute for spirituality. Many more could be discussed, but space forbids a detailed treatment of the ways Christians have expressed their faith in opposition to the spirituality taught by Jesus and His disciples.

The question is whether or not those who have falsely substituted erroneous beliefs for biblical spirituality can ever lay aside their beliefs and come to a knowledge of the truth.

For some it may be too late, especially for those who teach these substitutions. Myth sometimes becomes heresy, and heresy sometimes leads people out of God's kingdom altogether. It doesn't have to be this way, but pride often enters into the heart of man and convinces him that he or she has become so wise that they alone know the truth.

For those who will humble themselves before God it is never too late. Furthermore, understanding spirituality is not that difficult. But it does involve a study of the Bible with a mind that is willing to look at it with a fresh openness. It is, after all, Jesus Christ and His first century followers—not those who wrote and spoke in subsequent years—who understood spirituality with a God-given insight.

And any understanding of spirituality must begin with the teaching of Jesus that loving God and loving one's neighbor are more important than any other commands in the Bible.

Paul had much to say about the nature of spirituality in our lives, how the spirituality of our hearts yields an abundance of good works toward God and our fellow human beings. He tells the young Roman church:

> I appeal to you therefore, brethren, by the mercies of God, to present your bodies as a living sacrifice, holy and acceptable to God, which is your spiritual worship (Rom. 12:1).

In the rest of the chapter Paul exhorts his readers to attitudes and acts of Christian love reflecting the spirituality of lives humbly presented to God:

1. Attitudes:
   humility
   genuine love
   hatred of evil (not hatred of evil *people*)
   a hope that rejoices
   patience in tribulation
   constancy in prayer
   harmony with others

2. Acts of Service:
     contribution and aid
     acts of mercy
     be filled with the Spirit in serving
       the Lord
     practice hospitality
     bless those who persecute us
     live peaceably with all
     avoid vengeance
     give food and water to your enemies
     overcome evil with good

Elsewhere Paul tells us that as Christians we have been raised with Christ to the very throne of God. Therefore, we have the option as people of *free will* to set our minds on spiritual things, the things of God. He advises us:

> Put to death therefore what is earthly in you: fornication, impurity, passion, evil desire, and covetousness, which is idolatry. On account of these the wrath of God is coming. In these you once walked, when you lived in them. But now put them all away: anger, wrath, malice, slander, and foul talk from your mouth. Do not lie to one another, seeing that you have put off the old nature with its practices and have put on the new nature, which is being renewed in

knowledge after the image of the creator (Col. 3:1-10).

Some people think that putting *off* sin and putting *on* spirituality is difficult. It might be, but not if we sincerely invite Christ into our hearts and yield our lives to the God who called us to His Son.

When we do this, God gives us His Holy Spirit to help us and strengthen us.

Hans Küng reiterates the advice of Paul when he notes:

> Every Christian *is* a spiritual person . . .
> in as far as he has died to flesh and
> sin and has received the Spirit of God
> . . . . in as far as he can kill sin in his
> life and, by living in the Spirit, bring
> forth the fruit of the Spirit. [16]

The fruit of the Spirit is the result of allowing the Spirit of God to reign in our hearts. Paul tells the Colossians, as he also told the Ephesian and Galatian churches:

> Put on then, as God's chosen ones . . .
> compassion, kindness, lowliness
> meekness and patience and, if one
> has a complaint against another, forgiv-
> ing each other. As the Lord has
> forgiven you, so you also must forgive.

> And above all these put on love, which
> binds everything together in perfect
> harmony. And let the peace of Christ
> rule in your hearts, to which indeed
> you were called in the one body.
> And be thankful (Col. 3:12-15).

Here is a picture of the ideal Church, the Church that *can be* if we as individuals *want it to be.*

For the *real* Church belongs to Christ. It has received Jesus Christ into its very being, who is its source of salvation, strength, and wisdom, and it exists in union with Christ, in a life-long relationship of love and servanthood.

This is the Church which depends not upon human things to maintain itself, but upon the power of Christ and the Holy Spirit.

The Spirit was poured out upon the Church long ago when the apostle Peter preached the Church's first sermon on the Day of Pentecost. And the Spirit is continually poured out upon all who will yield their minds to Christ, to fill our hearts and lives with a spirituality that will enable us to share Christ with the world and to minister to the sick and the needy.

For those who have a hard time understanding this, who think that spirituality is found in "right belief" or the keeping of their church's laws, we can take heart knowing that Paul himself did not always understand this.

Before Paul met the risen Christ he was a Pharisee who worked hard to keep the letter of the law. But when he allowed Christ to come into his life, he found that true spirituality began in one's heart. Never could true spirituality penetrate a person from the outside.

This is why Paul could tell his fellow Jews:

> He is not a real Jew who is one outwardly, nor is true circumcision something external and physical. He is a Jew who is one inwardly, and real circumcision is a matter of the heart, spiritual and not literal. His praise is not from men but from God (Rom. 2:28-29).

This is the nature of the real Church, a Church to which both Catholics and Protestants belong through their common faith in Christ.

It is a Church which is neither Catholic nor Protestant, but merely Christian, believing in and following its Savior.

It is a Church which, though manifest outwardly toward others, is first of all one inwardly, spiritual, filled with love for God and love for all humanity.

What about sexual predators in the Church, you might be thinking. They're likely still out there, perhaps plotting their sinful acts even as I write these words. How can they be part of true Christian fellowship?

The Church, both Catholics and Protestants, cannot put up with these people, nor fellowship with those who persist in their sins. Adults and children should scream long and loud and fight when approached by them. And no one in authority should cover up the sins of these people, not even their best friends, but rather bring them to the light of Christ so that He might change their lives if they are willing. And, if appropriate, as Pope Francis has ordered, they must be reported to the local authorities.

And for those in the Church who have not been caught but still struggle with sexual deviance, bring yourself to Christ totally and completely. He will wash you clean by his love, and fill you with His power and with the power of the Holy Spirit to be a renewed person, a new creation.

The power of Christ can change anyone, no matter the depth of their perversion and unrighteousness.

Christ's spiritual calling to believers everywhere is powerful, joyful and peace-giving. It is His way of uniting believers from around the world, whether Catholic or Protestant, in the fellowship, love and joy of serving our great God.

6

Because God Loves Us, We Can Love and Respect One Another

There's never been a time that I haven't been in the Church. Some would say I was born into the Church, and in a sense that's true. My parents were Christians long before I was born, and my mother brought me for dedication to Christ when I was a baby. I was not baptized since the Disciples of Christ church we attended in San Francisco did not believe in infant baptism.

At the same time my mother secretly, and prayerfully, dedicated me to the ministry. She simply felt in her heart that God would one day call me into His work. While I was growing up, her prayers for me never ceased—especially when I voiced opposition to being a minister.

She didn't tell me about the dedication, and how she'd prayed about it for many years until I responded to God's calling in my early twenties.

For the first ten years of my life I knew nothing about other churches and persuasions. In 1946, when I was three years old, we moved to Los Angeles and attended Hollywood-Beverly Christian Church, in Hollywood, for the next seven years.

It was there I learned that God loved me, and not only me, but everybody. I never heard a thing about denominational squabbles and theological battles. At least I don't recall hearing anything negative in those formative years. It's a great tragedy of the Church that many children learn only a negative Christianity.

When I was nine years old I attended special classes at Easter and made the decision to accept Jesus Christ as my Savior. I was baptized (fully immersed) along with other kids my age and a few adults.

But things changed. My folks moved away from the Hollywood area and we attended an independent Christian church, one of many which had broken away from the Disciples of Christ near the turn of the century.

Suddenly I was hearing—more than occasionally—very negative sermons. These could be about most any subject, but the favorite seemed to be about baptism. I heard dozens of sermons condemning Lutherans, Presbyterians, Methodists, Catholics—especially Catholics—and anyone else to hell who had not been immersed when baptized. It did not seem to matter how much he or she believed in Christ.

Although I did learn about having faith in Christ, most ministers and laity alike preached long and loud on the necessity of immersion for salvation. Many people in the independent Christian church have gotten away from this hard-line position today.

But I can still see one angry, Arizona minister, his face and neck red with fire, his eyes violent, spewing out hatred for other denominations, naming them one by one.

I never did figure out why they preached so hard on the subject to people who were already immersed.

Fortunately for me, neither of my parents, although they believed in the New Testament practice of immersion, ever developed any animosity toward people of other churches. My father remained a Disciples of Christ supporter until he died, though he never attended one of their churches again.

My mother had attended the Congregational church as a child, and although she later believed that immersion was the proper New Testament form of baptism, she never held any prejudice against those who weren't immersed—not even the

Catholics who were dreaded and damned so often not only by the Christian church, but by other Protestants as well.

Whether it was my own parents' acceptance of Christians of other persuasions, or simply my own ability to think for myself and study the Bible for myself I'm not sure, but, like my parents, I never picked up on all the hate sermons I heard.

Of course, I never really believed that baptism all by itself could save anybody from their sins. Personal faith in Christ always seemed to me to speak more of a real relationship with God than any outward religious act.

One time a few of us smart high school graduates ganged up on our well-liked teacher of the college-career class and asked him how a person dying of thirst and dehydration in the middle of the desert could be baptized in water should he suddenly confess his sins and express faith in Christ. "God would find a way," we were told, but 1 don't think any of us accepted that as the answer to the impossibility of the situation.

Strangely, some of the people who preached long and hard on salvation by immersion believed in deathbed conversions. Perhaps they weren't as hard-line on the subject as they professed to be.

God's call to the ministry coincided with my decision to leave the independent Christian church. Despite my rejection of a negative theology on the part of some people, I will forever be grateful to their nurture during my adolescence. I am particularly indebted to a minister at high school youth camp one summer—whose name I will never know—who challenged me to study the Bible. At sixteen I responded to the challenge and have been studying the Bible ever since.

This is the precious variety that each tradition within Christ's Church has to offer—if we are willing to appreciate one another. People who love Christ are everywhere, and one will share with the Church what another has overlooked or forgotten.

I joined the Assemblies of God, where I was later ordained, because of their belief in a personal baptism in the Holy Spirit. The church I first attended was also more accepting of Christians from varied backgrounds and was heavily involved in the charismatic movement at the time. But I soon discovered that many in the denomination preached against other churches with a vigor that exceeded what I'd experienced in my teen years.

The wrath of some Assemblies of God people was directed toward other Christians for a different reason than that of the independent Christian church. No one in the Assemblies believed in baptismal regeneration. They were simply convinced that people in the historical churches, especially Catholics, couldn't have received Jesus Christ as their Savior because they were either too liberal, too Roman, or just too different.

I recall seeing an article in *The Pentecostal Evangel*, the official magazine of the denomination, plainly stating that the historical churches were the *weeds* in Jesus' parable of the weeds among the wheat (Matt. 13:24-30 and 36-43). The wheat, of course, was the newer, fundamentalist churches in America.

The article urged people to stay in the Assemblies, or, if you weren't already in a "Bible-believing" church, get in one fast. For when Jesus returned, which could be at any moment, all the weeds (the historical church people) would be cast into hell, just as the weeds in the parable would be burned at harvest time.

In all fairness to the Assemblies of God, many people in the denomination were angered by the denunciation, even some who were suspicious of other Christians. Among other things wrong with the article, it plainly violated Jesus' command not to judge the hearts of people we don't even know (Matt. 7:1-5).

Furthermore, many in the Assemblies of God, due either to life situations or ministries, were well aware that Christianity isn't limited to any one persuasion. *Christianity is where you find it.*

The late Rev. David du Plessis was one Assemblies of God minister who saw God at work in other churches. A descendant of the French Huguenots, he spent his early years as a fiery evangelist preaching little but sin, hell, and repentance. He wanted people, in his words, "to smell the sulfur from the flames of hell."

But God was working in his heart, and once he

really came to *know* the living Christ, not just believe in Him, he began to experience the love of God. He became an accepting person rather than a condemning person. Instead of trying to scare people into following Christ, he realized that God wanted him to love them into the kingdom of heaven.

Unlike some of his fellow ministers who castigated other churches, Rev. du Plessis spent many years attempting to bring Christians together in the love of Christ. His ministry took him even to Rome's Vatican, where he was always welcomed.

While I was still an Assemblies of God minister, my education took me to Pepperdine University in Malibu, California. I was somewhat leery of what I might find there because Pepperdine was founded by members of the non-instrumental church (no musical instruments allowed in worship services), the independent Churches of Christ, which was also an off-shoot of the Disciples of Christ.

The non-instrumental churches were generally more hard-line than the independent Christian church when it came to baptism. Like some splinter Baptist groups, some of these churches were adamant that you not only had to be immersed, but that you had to be immersed in *their* particular church to become a member.

But I didn't find any rabid fundamentalism at Pepperdine. What I did find was an openness to students who wanted to study the Bible. Since I was working on a master's degree in religion, I can't say what the entire school was like (Pepperdine has, in many respects, disassociated itself from any church affiliation). But I found the professors in the religion department to be fair to any student, regardless of denominational preference.

I especially appreciated their long-time professor of religion, Dr. Frank Pack, now retired, for his honesty, understanding, and appreciation for Christians and scholars of other churches, conservative though he was. Most of all, through our many talks and time spent in classes, I never knew him to be anything but a person who truly loved Jesus Christ and His Church.

One time a student—from what church I don't recall—asked Dr. Pack if it were true that the pope had the number 666 on his hat. (We all know what that number signifies!). This rumor has been circulating among Protestants for years. Dr. Pack smiled, shook his head in dismay, and assured the student that it wasn't true.

At the leading of God, my wife and I decided to join the Congregational Christian Churches while I was still at Pepperdine. Our first experience in a Congregational church was in Newport Beach, California, at Plymouth Congregational Church, where Rev. John Lindvall was the senior minister. Previously, he had been an Assemblies of God Army chaplain for twenty-seven years. He still ministers in the Assemblies of God, especially to chaplains, as well as in the Congregational church.

Rev. Lindvall founded and operates Mission Ministries, a low-overhead, inter-denominational missionary support group, which helps feed hungry people while sharing Christ through established missionaries.

When my wife and I walked into his church for the first time, we thought we were in heaven. We haven't had this same "heavenly" experience in every Congregational church, and have, in fact, experienced it in Catholic, Baptist, Episcopal, Lutheran, Presbyterian, Evangelical Free, and other churches as well.

The difference at Plymouth Congregational Church was simply that Chaplain John, as many call him, was a person who loved Christ and cared for others. He didn't see people as Baptist or Congregational, liberal or fundamental, and perhaps not as either saint or sinner. Anyone entering the church was considered a person of worth and value, a person whom God loves and for whom Christ died.

In this light of love, denominational preference and theological differences are of little importance.

After earning an M.A. in Religion at Pepperdine, I applied for a variety of ministerial positions. I wasn't sure what God wanted me to do. It turned out I was still learning.

Once I called a Catholic high school which had

placed an ad for a teacher in Religion. On the phone I was asked only one question: "Are you a Catholic?"

"No."

"Sorry. We hire Catholics only."

Probably I should have known that. But I keep hoping.

I called Southern California College, an Assemblies of God liberal arts college in Costa Mesa, California, where I had received a B.A. in Religion a few years prior. The chairman of the Department of Religion was glad to see me. (He had earned his doctorate at Notre Dame University—excellent biblical department, he said.) He hired me to teach just one New Testament class.

The dean told him to forget me. I was no longer an Assemblies of God minister. There was a rule.

At one point in time I thought about joining a larger body of Congregational churches, the United Church of Christ. This denomination is known for being blatantly liberal, yet there are many conservative Christians and ministers among them.

One of their senior ministers advised me not to do so. Another warned me that in the San Francisco Bay Area, at least, I would probably run into a roadblock of liberalism.

Probably I should have listened to them. But God was still teaching me about His Church. And I keep on hoping.

"No problem," the district pastor assured me the day I appeared before the ministerial committee.

"We're very inclusive. We don't want to keep you out."

"Sorry," the chairperson told me. "You're not really one of us."

Why wasn't I? Wasn't I a Christian minister? Didn't I care about people? Didn't I preach the gospel? Didn't I visit those sick and in prison and help those in need?

The ministerial committee never asked me any of these questions. They wanted to know only whether or not I agreed with them on several fad theologies circulating in liberalism.

I did not agree with them any more than I agreed with some of the fad theologies circulating in fundamentalism, and I carefully explained to them why I preferred to stick with New Testament Christianity.

Some of them were angered. They were looking for clones of themselves, ministers who thought like them and acted like them. They had no other criterion.

What is it about Church people, especially those on opposite extremes of the theological spectrum, that makes them so arrogant? What is it about Church people of varying denominational beliefs and practices that makes them so contentious?

Why don't Christians love and respect each other?

Jesus did His best to teach that God's people are those who love and forgive one another, those who work together, pray together, and worship together in harmony with God, being led by the Spirit, to present to the world a *single* Church united in love and witness.

But the Church has seldom been able to do this.

What's the problem? Why is it that people whose God and whose Savior love them deeply and teach them to do likewise cannot receive and reflect that love to people even of their own faith?

As I pointed out in the last chapter, the old excuse that "we're just human" won't work anymore. As Christians, as God's people, as servants of Jesus Christ, we not only have the Bible to guide us, but we have the Holy Spirit. Christians are a cut above "human."

We don't have to let human desires and ambitions of an ungodly and unholy sort rule our lives if we don't want to.

Perhaps this is just where the problem occurs. We don't want to do it God's way. And too often we refuse to admit or believe that we are not doing it God's way.

Billy Graham once said (actually, he's probably said it more than once!) that *pride* is the greatest of all human sins. Pride keeps us from thinking as we ought to think and doing as we ought to do.

Although there is a positive side of pride, the negative side is often quite destructive.

We see pride at work in the very early days of the Church, when the strict Hebrew Christians of

Jerusalem neglected some of the Hellenistic Hebrew Christians (Jews who had taken on Greek culture) in the daily distribution to the poor of food and clothing (Acts 6:1-7). The Orthodox Hebrews believed that they were better than the Hellenists in God's eyes.

The apostles stopped this practice immediately, but gradually, like a slowly advancing army, pride led to other forms of exclusiveness and division.

When pride takes over, love is shoved into the background of our lives. We bring it to the forefront only when we want to.

When pride takes over, we become self-righteous, puffed up in our own importance. We seldom recognize the importance of others and our role as servants of Christ.

In every generation throughout the Church's history, certain people have decided that they, and they alone, have discovered God's truths. Therefore, they conclude that it is their duty to silence the ignorant and the dissenters—anyone who doesn't agree with them.

We see this attitude coming to a head in the early fifth century on the part of no less an astute thinker than St. Augustine. Earlier in his ministry as the bishop of Hippo in North Africa, Augustine advocated leading people to Christ through love. However, after many years of disputing with the Donatists, a group which believed that the sacraments were invalid unless administered by holy men, Augustine decided that heretics could be compelled to conform through physical violence.

This is not what Jesus said. He spoke of love.

Nor is this what Paul said. He advised simply to admonish a heretic and, if he will not receive the truth, leave him to his own foolishness (Titus 3:9-11).

We are not, of course, necessarily discussing heresy here. There is such a thing as heresy, but it is not usually heresy which divides Christian brothers and sisters. Rather, it is the pride in each of us which convinces us that we are better than everyone else.

Once we convince ourselves that we are indeed God's wonderfully perfect people, we're overcome with the tendency to castigate those among us who are less than perfect, and disassociate ourselves from outsiders who contend with our "perfect" knowledge and "superior" modes of worship.

Even when our theology is correct, we do not have the right to be arrogant and contentious. This is what got Augustine into trouble. Clyde Manschreck comments on the destructive nature of Augustine's theory of dealing with dissent: "Augustine's arguments regarding compulsion passed into the medieval church, which readily sanctioned death now to save the soul from the future fires of hell, thus choking heretical dissent and preserving unity."[17]

In 1199 Pope Innocent III declared heresy a capital crime. Beginning in 1233, the Inquisition was used with the cooperation of civil courts to silence anyone who disagreed with Rome. In 1542 it was applied to Protestants.

Many Protestants were killed for their beliefs even outside of the Inquisition, especially in France and England. Some days they died by the thousands.

Protestants quickly decided that if killing was good for the church in Rome, it would be good for them, too. They killed not only Catholics, but fellow Protestants, notably the peace-loving Anabaptists in the sixteenth century over theological and sociological differences.

In John Calvin's attempt at theocracy in Geneva in the sixteenth century, adulterers, witches, blasphemers, heretics, and traitors were all sentenced to death, the most famous of which was John Servetus, whose "crime" was disagreement with both Catholic and Protestant theology.

The idea of killing dissenters spilled over into the New World only mildly. Those who trusted God by crossing the vast Atlantic on their tiny sailing ships were tiring of the bloodshed they had left behind.

But the dissension and name-calling has never stopped. Now we "kill" and destroy each other with written and spoken words.

It doesn't have to be this way.

Yes We Can Love One Another!

We can end the bitterness and strife if we want to.

But we first have to believe that it is our obligation — really, the essence of Christianity — to love each other. When we begin to love each other we begin to listen to each other and understand each other. We won't necessarily agree completely with each other, but we can at least respect each other on the basis of the common faith we have in Christ Jesus.

But the process must begin with love.

Why is it that we don't love? Why is it that even Christians who say they deeply believe in Christ and in the Bible often show no love to those who disagree with them?

The answer is simply that although they have given mental assent to following Christ, they have never allowed Christ to fully enter their hearts.

For Jesus Christ is God's message of love to the world, and Christ is Himself love.

To know Christ is to know God's love.

To be *in* Christ is to be *in* love.

It is impossible to know in a personal way a love that is found only in God and His Son and not love our fellow human beings in return.

This was the experience of those who followed Jesus in the first century. They gave their lives for Christ and for their fellow human beings because they loved others. Virtually every letter in the New Testament in some way or another tells us to love one another, for Christ has loved us.

The words of Paul ring loud and true to those of us who are divided in the twentieth century Church:

> Be kind to one another, tenderhearted, forgiving one another, as God in Christ forgave you . . . And walk in love, as Christ loved us and gave himself up for us, a fragrant offering and sacrifice to God (Eph. 4:32-5:2).

Peter also addressed the problem of strife among those who follow Christ:

> All of you, have unity of spirit, sympathy, love of the brethren, a tender heart and a humble mind. Do not return evil for evil or reviling for reviling; but on the contrary bless, for to this you have been called, that you may obtain a blessing (1 Peter 3:8-9).

There's really no joy, no gain, no purpose in quarreling. But when we love we have God's blessing.

John's language is even stronger. Lack of love is an alienation from God. But when we love one another we can experience God's daily presence. He advises:

> Beloved, let us love one another; for love

> is of God, and he who loves is born of God and knows God. He who does not love does not know God; for God is love. In this the love of God was made manifest among us, that God sent his only Son into the world, so that we might live through him. In this is love, not that we loved God but that he loved us and sent his Son to be the expiation for our sins. Beloved, if God so loved us, we also ought to love one another. No man has ever seen God; if we love one another, God abides in us and his love is perfected in us (1 John 4:7-12).

To be in Christ is to know and share God's love.

The Church was founded to be a witness of Jesus Christ as an instrument of God's love to the world.

The real Church understands this and has, even throughout history in the Church's bloodiest days, practiced love. The Church that forgets to love, or refuses to love, is no Church at all.

But we do not have to be a loveless Church. Whether Catholic or Protestant, we can let the words of Paul from the Bible's love chapter burn fiercely in our hearts:

> If I have prophetic powers, and understand all mysteries and all knowledge, and if I have all faith, so as

to remove mountains, but have not love,
I am nothing (1 Cor. 13:2).

And we can put into practice toward one another, regardless of our beliefs and practices, the hallmark of our faith in Jesus Christ:

Love bears all things, believes all things, hopes all things, endures all things (1 Cor. 13:7).

When we make the conscious decision to love, when we truly believe that God loves all people, not just ourselves; when we decide that the common bond of all Christians is both our faith in Jesus Christ and the love He showed for us in His death for our sins, we, the people who are the Church, will undergo an amazing transformation.

No longer will we see doctrine, liturgy, polity, or anything else as grounds for hatred, accusations, dissension, anathemas, and ostracism. For our faith in Jesus Christ, coupled with God's love in our hearts, forms a bond stronger than even a significant difference can rupture.

No longer will we be suspicious and distrustful of those who don't look like us, think like us, or act like us.

No longer will we think that our particular church is better than everyone else's, even though we prefer it.

Rather, our love for others and our appreciation for their faith in Christ Jesus, though it may be expressed in a way foreign to us, will open our hearts to understanding and respecting Christians of other traditions.

This is not as difficult as it might seem.

When Paul wrote to the Philippian church, he asked them to "complete my joy by being of the same mind, having the same love, being in full accord and of one mind. Do nothing from selfishness or conceit, but in humility count others better than yourselves" (2:2-3).

The Greek city of Philippi was founded by the father of Alexander the Great, and in the time of Paul it was a Roman colony. It was home to Greeks, Romans, and Jews. The account of Paul's missionary work at Philippi in Acts and his letter to the new congregation both indicate that this was a church where people of all three cultures worshiped.

Although Romans and Jews had to some extent taken on Greek customs, there nevertheless remained differences in dress, culture, and language. But the Christians at Philippi put aside these differences through their common bond of love and faith in Jesus Christ.

When we, as Christians of a multi-cultural age and multi-denominational churches, begin to love, we realize that in Christ we can find the love to count others as people better than ourselves.

And when we do this, differences—even theological differences—become less important than our common faith in Christ and our common goal to share Christ with the world.

After all, God neither calls us nor expects us to think and act alike.

Does it really matter if we don't agree on all points of theology?

Does it really matter if some of us like Gaither's music, others prefer the old hymns, and still other like Bach?

Does it really matter if some wear three-piece suits or hats and gloves to church while others wear blue jeans?

Does it really matter if some ministers wear no robes while others wear black robes, and still others white or red and large hats?

Does it really matter if some churches have a highly structured liturgy, while others conduct a very informal service?

It is true that we cannot have genuine fellowship with those who profess Christ with their lips but deny Him with their unchristian actions. Nor can we fellowship with those who purport to be Christians, but who no longer believe that Christ is God's Son and the world's Savior.

But too often the things which separate us are the non-essentials, the petty little differences which God couldn't care less about.

What God is concerned about is our hearts.

And when we love from our hearts, and concentrate on the things which unite us, then that common faith which we have in Jesus Christ will transcend any differences we might have.

Indeed, if the Church is to survive as a visible entity in today's troubled world, it *must* come together around the love of Christ.

Hans Küng and Walter Kasper share this insightful comment by Ronald Modras on the importance of fellowship:

> No less than any other community, a church characterized by pluralism, if it is to survive, must be founded upon a consensus, a common bond, a sense of loyalty that surpasses all other differences. Churches distinguished from one another by divergence can overcome their divisions only in terms of such a superseding loyalty. For Christians, the object of their loyalty, their ultimate source of unity, cannot be a doctrine, a set of rituals, or a system of organization. *The fundamental source of unity* for the Church today, the ultimate object of its loyalty, *can be only the person and cause of Jesus and the conviction that he is Christ and Lord.*[18]

There will always be those in the Church who will resist the fellowship of Christians outside their own denomination. It's a sad fact of Church life that some Catholics will always dislike Protestants, some Protestants will always dislike Catholics, and some Protestants will always dislike other Protestants. (There are some Catholics who dislike other Catholics, but this is usually cultural.)

Sometimes this is so simply because we conform to the crowd we run with.

A young couple who came to me to be married seemed like the sweetest pair until the prospective groom blurted how nervous he was about getting married. The prospective bride seemed a little surprised until he explained that all of his friends who had gotten married were now divorced. He was afraid the same thing would happen to him, and he didn't want that.

I suggested that perhaps his friends were quickly divorced because they placed no value on marriage but viewed it as a temporary convenience easily scuttled.

He conceded that I was probably right, but what could he do?

"You don't have to think like your friends," I assured him. "God gave you a brain of your own. Your marriage can be permanent if you want it to be—if you honor the sanctity of marriage. Don't let your friends influence you."

The last I heard, he and his wife were still happily married.

So it can be with the Church. Catholics and

Protestants can love one another, share together, and work together if we want to, and if we really value the institution of the Church and the permanency of our relationship to God.

When we get our eyes on Jesus Christ, on the one who unites us, instead of on what divides us, then we can be the truly great Church that God intended, a single Church united in love and in the power of the Holy Spirit throughout the entire world.

We can be the Church Christ prayed we would be.

Here is the greatest challenge and call still facing the Church of today.

7

Sharing the Joy as Servants of Jesus Christ

No one could remember how long he'd been sitting by the roadside on the outskirts of Jericho, basket in hand, leaning against a large, spreading palm tree for the little shade it provided from the incessant sun, and begging. There was nothing else he could do in life—just beg.

Day after weary day he came and sat and begged.

Everyone knew him. Bartimaeus was his name. He was the son of Timaeus, and he was blind. There was nothing else wrong with him—just blind. Many blind men became beggars in Jesus' day.

This one just sat there, the passing oxen and

157

their wagons, the heavily-laden donkeys and the passers-by on foot hurrying to and from Jerusalem, kicking up wisps of dust that floated over and covered him from head to toe by day's end.

But there was something different about this morning. Jericho was ablaze with excitement. Bartimaeus had sensed it even before he settled into the depression beneath his palm tree. It was almost Passover, his father had told him, excitement enough as nearly everyone in town always journeyed to Jerusalem.

But there was something else. The teacher all of Palestine was talking about had come to Jericho. He too was on His way to attend the Passover. Jesus was His name, and some said He was the Messiah, the promised Son of David, the Savior promised by God through the prophets long ago.

After all, He could do miracles. Crowds had followed Him all the way down the Jordan Valley from across the Jordan River. He would stop to teach as they walked, and then He would bless the children and pray for the sick. Why, He could even cast out demons, restoring men and women to their right minds.

Was it true? Bartimaeus wondered. *Maybe . . . maybe Jesus could open his eyes!* Or would He even care to be seen with a wretched, blind beggar? Nobody paid much attention to him anymore—not since he was a little boy.

Suddenly he heard it—the chattering and scuffling of a crowd coming his way. This was not the usual tumult of those on their way to Passover. There was something else . . .

Their voices grew louder. This was a happy crowd, an eager crowd — as though they expected something exciting to happen. Maybe it was *Him* — this one some thought was the Messiah.

"What's happening?" Bartimaeus cried out, unable to contain himself any longer. "Who's coming?"

"It's the teacher," an unfamiliar voice said to him, "the one named Jesus, from Nazareth."

It was Him! This was his chance to be healed! If only he could somehow get to Jesus through the multitude. *I'll call to Him,* he thought. *I'll never push my way through the crowd. What chance would a blind man have?*

"Jesus, Son of David!" he cried. "Have mercy on me!"

"Shut up!" someone yelled at him. "Leave the teacher alone. Let Him teach."

"That's just Bartimaeus," a familiar voice said. "Be quiet, Bartimaeus. Jesus doesn't have time for you."

No! He couldn't be quiet! "Jesus, Son of David! Have mercy on me!"

All of a sudden it was still. He heard a voice in the distance, like someone calling. Then another voice shouted, "Bartimaeus! Take heart. Rise, and come. Jesus is calling to you."

This was his day! Jesus would touch him and open his eyes! Instantly he leaped to his feet.

Several hands took his arms and led him to Jesus down the road.

"What do you want me to do for you?" a voice asked.

Bartimaeus knew it was Jesus, for this man spoke like no one he'd ever heard, a voice of authority and confidence, yet a voice of love and concern.

The vacant, pleading, yet hopeful eyes stared at Jesus. "Master, let me receive my sight."

Jesus said to him, "Go your way; your faith has made you well."

He could see! He could see! "Praise God!" Bartimaeus said, lifting his eyes to the blue of the morning skies. "Wait! I, too, will come to the Passover, to praise God for the miracle of my sight!"

Some people think Bartimaeus received his sight as a further demonstration that Jesus was indeed the promised Messiah of Israel. For Jesus was on His way to Jerusalem for what He knew would be an ignominious death. There was not much time left for His short, public ministry.

Although the opening of a blind person's eyes is miraculous, Jesus likely would have chosen something more spectacular than the healing of eyes, and someone more important than a tattered, blind beggar—if verification of His power and authority had been His motivation for this miracle. Plenty of political figures were ill or crippled in those days. Why not heal one of them?

One cannot read this story, however, without feeling the great *compassion* of Jesus. He healed Bartimaeus because He cared for him, because he was a person in need, and because, despite all the obstacles placed in front of him, he came to Jesus for help.

This beautiful story from Mark 10:46-52 is not so much an example of God's power resident in Jesus Christ as it is a demonstration of God's *caring* nature. For we see in Jesus—the one who revealed God to us more clearly—someone who truly cared for humankind. He came in God's love to share the grace, salvation, blessings, and power of God with all who sought Him.

Jesus was not just a hearer and a teacher of God's word, but a doer. His life and ministry were motivated by *compassion,* by a desire to give comfort and help to those who were oppressed by the harsh realities of life.

Jesus Christ was both a servant of God and a servant of humanity. His apostles did not always understand His status as God's servant. Nor did they expect to be His servants in the strictest meaning of the word.

James and John, in fact, asked Jesus for special places of authority when He established His kingdom. The request was out of order first of all because Jesus never intended to establish an earthly kingdom. The request was also out of order because no true follower of Jesus would ever *be* served.

Rather, just as Jesus was a servant of God, so would anyone who honestly followed Him be servants of God.

Jesus answered this request with an observation that is applicable to those who would believe in Him in every age:

> "Whoever would be great among you must be your servant, and whoever would be first among you must be slave of all. For the Son of Man [Jesus Himself] also came not to be served but to serve, and to give his life as a ransom for many" (Mark 10:43-45).

What kind of servant was Jesus?

We see the nature of His servanthood in His willingness to minister to Bartimaeus.

Mark tells us "a great multitude followed Jesus." We don't know for sure how many people that was. However, since the multitude was likely going up to Jerusalem to attend the Passover, there were probably several hundred people walking along with Jesus and His disciples.

When Bartimaeus called to Jesus, He may well have been sharing the wisdom that flowed from His soul. How easy it would have been for Him to ignore that call from the distance. People were calling to Him all the time. Could He afford to take the time for this one, someone He could not even see?

These thoughts run through our heads all the time when someone we don't know comes to us, even in need, and makes a demand on our time.

But these thoughts did not run through Jesus' head. The cry of Bartimaeus needed to be answered. It was a cry of faith, but it was also a desperate cry. Jesus could not refuse him, even if it meant—as it did—working His way through the crowd and delaying the wearisome, uphill, seventeen-mile journey to Jerusalem.

Although it is the rare Christian today who would not claim to be a servant of Christ just as Jesus was a servant of God, we do not always see the same level of servanthood that Jesus demonstrated on the outskirts of Jericho.

Rather, it is the complaint of many who attend church services today that the local churches often ignore them as individuals. If you want to see the pastor in some churches, you have to go to his house—and even then you probably won't find him home. Many pastors don't even visit the sick to share the Scriptures and to pray for God's comforting touch and healing power. This is true not only of large congregations, but small congregations as well.

Ministers are simply "too busy." This contention will not be denied, but the question is "How are they too busy?"

The business of Jesus was sharing salvation and life and health with those in need. Too often this is *not* what a pastor is busy doing.

I was told the story of two ministers who held a weekend seminar. After the seminar many people sought them on a personal basis for counseling and prayer. One minister refused to meet with anyone. "I'm not getting paid for that," he said on his way out the door.

The other minister stayed and shared what God gave him—until the last person had been ministered to late on a Sunday afternoon.

This story illustrates what is happening in the Church today. Time, outside interests, and money—or sometimes the lack of it—take too many people away from serving the Christ who freely stopped and helped those in need.

Jesus was happy being a servant of God.

Why aren't Christians happy to be servants of Jesus Christ?

We also see in this story of Bartimaeus Jesus' great love for the least of society's members. Mark tells us that many people tried to get Bartimaeus to be quiet. After all, Jesus was now a person of renown, with people hounding Him day and night. Why would He want to stop for a poor, blind beggar by the side of the road?

But the cries of Bartimaeus could not be stilled by the crowd around him. They probed the depths of Jesus' heart. He could not pass him by.

Jesus came to serve, not to be served. That is why even the Pharisees, most of whom were jealous of Him, readily noticed His lack of respect for men of position. "Teacher," they said, "we know that you are true, and teach the way of God truthfully, and care for no man; for you do not regard the position of men" (Matt. 22:15-16).

It was not that Jesus had no use for politicians or religious leaders. He would have gladly served them also, and a few of them He did. The problem was that people of status often have little use for those who do not respect their positions in life.

God's way is to respond with love to those who truly seek Him. A person's social standing has no command of God's love and no bearing on His response.

During the years that I pastored in the Los Angeles area, our church supported a missionary to South America. Whenever he was in the States he and his wife would stop by. One Sunday morning they showed up on short notice.

"I suppose we should be over at the big church politicking," he said, grinning. The "big" church across town was *thirty* times our size. "But we'd rather be here where God wants us today."

Our congregation loved them. They always blessed us by their ministry. And, for our small church, they always received the generous support of our offerings and our prayers.

A fellow minister once pastored a small congregation on the central California coast. Many missionaries were invited to go there and speak, but only a few went. Most declined the invitation when they found out the size of the congregation. What they didn't know was that one member of the church *always* made out a very large check to any missionary who came by and shared his or her heart while on furlough.

I'm not knocking "big" churches. I've ministered in large churches. They do many things small churches cannot begin to accomplish for Christ.

The point is that God does not respect the things which often earn the respect of human beings. God respects the heart. He ministers to the cries of anyone who sincerely seeks Him. This was why Jesus ministered to Bartimaeus when the villagers thought he wouldn't be interested.

The Church has not always understood or practiced this radical form of servanthood.

Paul understood it. He lived the life of Christ — for him a life of suffering — in order to minister to others.

It was not simply through Paul's time spent in the Arabian desert alone with God that he developed the spirit of a true servant. It was, rather, due in part to the love which was shown him by other Christians after he came to Christ on the Damascus road.

A disciple by the name of Ananias, who lived in Damascus and likely would have been thrown into prison by Paul had he completed his intended vengeful plans, cared enough to take Paul into his home and minister to his physical and spiritual needs even though Paul's reputation as a bitter and violent persecutor of the Church scared him.

Ananias was a servant of God. He listened to God. And God assured him that Paul was His chosen servant, who would share the gospel with both Jew and Gentile.

Paul discovered very early in his new life in Christ that, although his new Christian friends were people of varying social backgrounds, their common *bond* was a bold faith in Christ. And their common *practice* was caring for one another and for those outside the Christian community.

Soon Paul came to say of both himself and his new friends in Christ, "This is how one should regard us, as servants of Christ and stewards of the mysteries of God" (1 Cor. 4:1). (Paul uses the phrase "mysteries of God" to refer to God's love and nature as revealed in Jesus Christ for Jew and Gentile alike.)

Believers in Christ are servants of Christ. A servant of Christ is one who cares for others because Christ cared for others.

You cannot read the life of Jesus in the Gospels, nor understand the life of Paul through his letters and Luke's narrative of his travels in Acts, without realizing the *joy* they found in serving God by serving others.

Were their lives difficult? Yes.

Were their lives physically harsh? Yes.

Were their lives denials of self? Yes.

But they were happy in their ministries. In the very depths of their souls the joy of serving God kept their spirits alive despite the bleak realities of the burdens placed upon them by those who chose to persecute them to their ultimate deaths.

Jesus and Paul gladly and willingly humbled themselves before God that they might fulfill God's calling on their lives to be His servants.

The Church has often found this same kind of humility difficult.

But humility is the mark of a true servant. For a servant of Christ does not consider himself or herself to be a better human being than others. Nor does a servant ignore the needs of others, for a servant is ready and willing to minister to others and to share with those in need.

The person who would truly follow Christ must be a servant of Christ by a denial of self, by humbly putting others first. Jesus both cautioned and observed:

> "He who loves his life loses it, and he who hates his life in this world will keep it for eternal life. If any one serves me, he must follow me; and where I am, there shall my servant be also. If any one serves me, the Father will honor him" (John 12:25-26).

The Church was intended to be a servant of

Jesus Christ in humility and love, denying itself so that it might share the love and abundance of God with the world: the good news of salvation in Jesus Christ, physical and emotional healing for the sick, food and clothing for the poor; and comfort, hope and faith for those discouraged in their spirits.

We also see in this story of Bartimaeus—as indeed we can understand from every story of Jesus' life in the Gospels—that Jesus had no interest in *politics.* The good news He brings concerns individual people. It has nothing to do with politics.

The closest Jesus came to even commenting on anything political was when He answered the Pharisees' question, "Is it lawful to pay taxes to Caesar, or not?"

The expected answer seems to be, "No, according to the laws of God you're not required to pay Rome's taxes." But that wasn't the answer Jesus gave. He showed them a Roman coin with Caesar's profile on it (probably Tiberius Caesar) and said, "Render to Caesar the things that are Caesar's, and to God the things that are God's" (Matt. 22:17-22).

It was right to pay the state's tax levy. Furthermore, God had made no law concerning state taxes. Jesus implied by His answer that religion and politics don't mix.

Yet some in the Church today are striving to turn it into the servant of politics, and its members into stewards of the mysteries of politics.

This is not to say that Christians shouldn't be involved in politics. Indeed, they should. Christian influence can and should be felt in every aspect of life.

But the Church can never be political in *nature.* For if it were to become a political power in the world — at any level of government — *it would cease to be the Church,* which can never be anything but a servant of Jesus Christ and a steward of the mysteries of God.

Curiously, fundamentalism, at least in the United States, is now asserting itself as a power in the political arena. This is the same fundamentalism which has long criticized liberalism for its involvement in politics. Politics is even being preached from fundamentalist pulpits to the joy of some and the amazement of others.

Liberalism, of course, has long been involved in politics. Political sermons are the order of the day in some churches. Politics is often preached, interspersed with a few verses from the Bible, as though it is God's agenda for human affairs.

This is, of course, a delusion, for *God has no political agenda.*

This is borne out by the fact that wherever politics is preached, God is shoved out of the picture entirely. I've heard political sermons in Congregational churches, Methodist churches, and Catholic churches. I didn't hear anything about God and my relationship to Him.

Some friends of ours who were raised Catholic and often attended a Catholic church never heard anything but South American politics preached there. They started attending a Methodist church when they moved to another town and again heard little but politics from the pulpit.

One day they realized that their church experiences were devoid of God and the spiritual life they so much wanted to hear about and participate in when they attended church.

Liberation theology, a propagation of Latin American Catholic theologians, which has been espoused by both Catholic and Protestant liberalism in the United States, is exemplary of what happens when Christ and the Church are politicized. Although this new theology addresses some real issues, namely poverty and oppression, it fails to be a servant of Christ—or even Christian—when it blends Marxism and Christianity and equates this syncretism with spirituality and salvation. Richard Neuhaus observes:

> The most extreme and candid statement of politicized religion is "liberation theology," notably, but not exclusively, in Latin America. Its proponents do not hesitate to equate salvation and "solidarity with the oppressed against the oppressor." The new dogma of liberation

theology reads: outside the class struggle there is no salvation.[19]

When Jesus Christ is politicized, He is no longer the Jesus of the Gospels, the Savior of the world.

When the Church is politicized, it is no longer the servant of Christ, sharing the good news of God's love.

A classic example of the Church overcome with the suffocating attempt to be a servant of Christ through politics is the support (sometimes monetary) often given to oppressive governments by Church people. Not surprisingly, fundamentalists often support right-wing oppressors, while liberals commend Marxist governments. Two recent examples: A few fundamentalist ministers gave their "blessing" to former apartheid leaders in South Africa, while at the same time a few liberal ministers journeyed to Nicaragua and "blessed" now-deposed Marxist leader Daniel Ortega.

If theology and polity have divided the Church, politics will divide it even more. For, when it comes to the cause of arguments between any two human beings, politics is definitely king.

Some people in the Church become angry and defensive when the Church's excursion into politics is criticized. They think the Church can and should be a legitimate political force in the world. They say this because for them politics is more important than spirituality. Their joy is not in sharing God's love with others, but in doing battle in the political arena.

Politics is more important than Jesus Christ Himself.

Protestants especially, however, overlook their own criticism of the Catholic church's joint ruling with kings and queens in the Middle Ages and on into the Reformation and Counter-Reformation periods. The Church became so political in Europe and in England's Reformation that it was scarcely recognizable as Christ's Church.

When the Church becomes a political force it is no longer the Church of the New Testament, which eschewed politics to serve Christ.

If the Church were to become political today, who would address the problem of spirituality in the lives of human beings? Who would share Christ with a lost world?

Our educational systems will not do it.

Private business will not do it.

Government will not do it.

Nobody will do it.

The Church can never be what man makes of it. It can be only what God makes of it, and God has made it a *spiritual* kingdom.

He has given the Church no political mandate because the Church is not political in nature.

The real Church—the Church of the future as well as the past—is spiritual in nature, a collective of believers in Jesus Christ who consider themselves His servants, who care for others, spiritual people who share the reality of God's love with the world through whatever gifts of service God has given them in the Holy Spirit's power.

Christians who are tempted or pressured by others to focus the Church's energies on politics should realize that this means abandonment of their spiritual mission in a world that desperately needs the spiritual dimension that the Church has to give.

When Jesus began His ministry in Galilee it was not politics He preached, but the *gospel of God.* Deliberately shunning politics, He freely offered help to those in physical and spiritual need. Shortly before He returned to His Father in heaven, He commanded His disciples to continue the work He had started:

> "Thus it is written, that the Christ should suffer and on the third day rise from the dead, and that repentance and forgiveness of sins should be preached in his name to all nations, beginning from Jerusalem. You are witnesses of these things" (Luke 24:46-48).

From that very first sermon Peter preached on the Day of Pentecost, sharing the message of the good news of Jesus Christ has been the spiritual mission of the Church Christ founded. It has no other mandate.

Furthermore, those first disciples found great joy and happiness in serving Christ. Following Peter's first sermon, when three thousand people received Christ as their Savior, Luke tells us that "they devoted themselves to the apostles' teaching and fellowship, to the breaking of bread and the prayers."

Wonders and signs were done through the apostles, bringing freedom and joy to every life God touched.

"All who believed" sold many possessions and distributed goods to others who had needs.

They worshiped together in the temple and in homes.

They ate together "with glad and generous hearts, praising God and having favor with all the people."

Many people in Jerusalem saw their great joy and happiness and came to receive Christ "day by day" (Acts 2:42-47).

What a happy Church! Yes, it was a tiny Church at this point in history. But tiny or not, these people were thrilled to find a new life in Christ and, in turn, share that new life with others, not only in a spiritual way, but in meeting the physical needs of their new friends.

A few years later, when persecution was beginning to scatter the young Church and Paul and Barnabas were carrying the good news of

Christ around the Mediterranean area, Luke reports that the disciples were still "filled with joy and with the Holy Spirit" (Acts 13:48-52).

The joy and happiness of these first disciples was not exaggerated by Luke, nor should it be underestimated by us today. There is no other explanation for the success of the first century Church in the face of stiff opposition from many segments of society.

As discussed in the first chapter, the joy and love of the Church began to wane in the second century for a number of reasons. As the deterioration of the Church of purity and harmony began, discord and strife led to the pursuit of unchristian theologizing and practices. This, in turn, led to the divisions in the Church, divisions which are still the cause of both old and new disputes.

Is it any wonder that Christians aren't happy serving Christ? Too often we let our squabbles get in the way of our service to Christ and to our ministries to our fellow human beings.

Too often the reason Christians are not happy serving Christ is that they have *never* truly served Him in any tangible way. In many cases it is not that they wouldn't do so, but only because the voices of strife or the cares or interests of life have drowned out that first century call of Christ, which comes to us yet today if we are willing to hear His voice: "Follow me!"

There is hope. Despite the disharmony in the Church today, many Christians, Catholics and Protestants alike, do love and appreciate one another and work together in the joy and happiness of the Lord. They understand that a servant of Christ is not one who thinks exactly like them, but one who believes in Christ Jesus and who follows Him wherever He leads.

In the small community on the outskirts of Los Angeles where I pastored in the early 70s, there was a grand total of three churches: Lutheran, American Baptist, and the independent church where I ministered, which had been founded mostly by Presbyterians (I was an Assemblies of God minister at the time).

It was the first full-time senior pastorate for each of us ministers. Perhaps that was why, even though we represented divergent traditions, we shared with one another occasionally and joined together for an Easter sunrise service each year. None of us considered ourselves better than anyone else, or our churches superior to the other two. We never experienced difficulty planning the Easter service, never any hogging of choice parts, never any doubt as to what the other fellow believed. We simply shared a common faith and brought forth an enriching sunrise service each year.

I like to think we got along well because we considered ourselves merely fellow servants of

Christ and our churches merely local fellowships of the worldwide Church.

Another story of Christian harmony is told by former Middle East hostage David Jacobsen, who refers to himself as "a Christian believer." While being held captive in Lebanon, he and four other hostages held worship services *twice daily* in the "Church of the Locked Door." Worshiping with him were two Catholics, Associated Press correspondent Terry Anderson and Reverend Lawrence Jenco, a priest; and two Presbyterians, Tom Sutherland of the American University, and Reverend Benjamin Weir, a minister.

Although these men were from divergent traditions and backgrounds and often held lively and acrimonious debates on matters of religion and philosophy (especially Jacobsen and Anderson), Jacobsen termed their worship "a true ecumenical brotherhood."[20]

Much of the reason for their willingness to worship together was their need for the strength and courage and spiritual uplift which they freely gave to one another. Throughout his book, Jacobsen cites the worship services as a major factor in getting him through the ordeal.

But I have to believe that part of their unity — even in the midst of religious and traditional Catholic-Protestant arguments — was because they considered themselves brothers in Christ; therefore all were fellow servants of Christ.

It is just this sort of mutual love and respect that was the mark of the first century Church. This is the Church which is *happy* serving Jesus Christ. This is the Church of the future.

Along this line, Protestants need to realize that Catholics don't need to drop their adoration of Mary — most of them won't anyway — before we can accept them as fellow servants of Jesus Christ. (My Catholic friends tell me they don't worship Mary as many Protestants believe.) Nor do they need to drop other traditions and practices which Protestants find objectionable but not offensive to God or contrary to Christianity (the sale of indulgences in the Middle Ages was both an offense to God and an unchristian exploitation of one's fellow citizens).

Protestants need to come to the place of discovery, the realization that we have a common history and a common bond with the Catholic Church: a shared belief in Jesus Christ and a shared conviction that we are His servants, called and commissioned by God to minister to the sinful and the suffering people of this world.

The Catholic Church, on the other hand, needs to realize that Protestants are never going to yield to its self-proclaimed authority as the "head" of all Christendom. The Catholic Church is not the Mother Church or the "true" church, for *there is no such institution and never was.* It exists only spiritually — in the hearts of all who believe in Jesus Christ.

Eastern Orthodox churches, especially those from ancient Mediterranean communities, are as historic as the Roman church, dating from Paul's missionary journeys in the mid-first century. Yet Orthodox churches have never yielded to Rome's claim to primacy. They would, however, gladly welcome the Catholic Church as an *equal* member in the Church universal (Protestants desirous of unity in servanthood would agree with this position).

Writing from the perspective of the Greek Orthodox Church, Demetrios J. Constantelos comments:

> The development of the Roman primacy was one of the major causes of the schism between the Latin West and the Greek East, and it continues to be a stumbling block for the reunion of Christendom, since it has become an element of the doctrinal teaching of the Roman Catholic faith . . . As long as the Roman Catholic Church teaches the supremacy in authority and power of the bishop of Rome over all Christendom, there is little hope for progress in the ecumenical dialogue on the reunion of the Churches. The Orthodox Church would have no hesitation in accepting the bishop of Rome as the first among equals.[21]

The primacy of the Roman Catholic Church

is still the official position of the Vatican, although it has recognized other Christian traditions since the Second Vatican Council in the 1960s. Because of this official posture some Protestants will have nothing to do with Catholics.

However, many Catholics and Protestants, individuals who are open to the love and humility of Christ, the attitudes of true servanthood, choose to ignore "official" positions. They have already discovered that Catholics and Protestants really do share a common faith and so are one in heart and mind.

The Church of the late twentieth century can be united by *a mutual love and respect* if it wants it.

It can have *God's love* if it wants it.

It can have the *mind of Jesus Christ* if it wants it.

It can have the *Holy Spirit's power* if it wants it.

It can have *divine wisdom, peace, and harmony* if it wants it.

It can have the *joy and happiness of serving Christ* if it wants it.

But to have these things—the blessings of participation in the real Church—it will have to humbly seek God for them instead of running on the lean fuel of purely human ways.

It will have to seek the *God of the Bible* and not the God of human philosophy.

It will have to seek the wisdom and love of the *Jesus of the Gospels*—the Jesus of both faith and history — and not the Jesus of human invention.

It will have to seek the *purity of the Scriptures* and not the polluted theology of human thinking.

It will have to come to the place of *acceptance* for all who sincerely and faithfully name the name of Jesus regardless of color, culture, or form of worship.

It will have to realize that while sexual abuse in its midst cannot be overlooked and must be honestly dealt with before God, it does not define Christ's universal Church filled with believers from every nation, village, and tongue.

Some people think the Church is dying. Others see it as totally irrelevant. Neither perspective is true, although many of us within the Church do long for the day when the highly-visible elements of the Church which do not honestly represent Christ are dead and buried forever.

The truth is that although the forces of history and time have chipped away at it, the Church founded by Jesus Christ and His disciples so long ago, the Church which serves Christ by serving humanity in love, is still very much alive. At times outside forces have reduced it to a whimper. On other occasions it has nearly destroyed itself. In our modern period forces both from within and without tear at it, threatening to drag it down into oblivion.

But the Church belongs to Christ and to those of faith in Him. As long as there are people on the face of the earth who lift their hearts to experience the God who created them, there will be people who believe in Christ and serve Him with gladness of heart.

Yet the Church of the future will have to resist the pressures that threaten to destroy it, especially negative, dogmatic theology from its right flank, and unbelief from its left flank. Furthermore, it will have to determine to be a loving servant of Jesus Christ and a living sacrifice in the service of God no matter what the non-Christian world thinks of it or does to it.

Most of all, it will have to be a Church which is not first and foremost either Catholic or Protestant but simply — yet powerfully--*Christian*.

I'm still hopeful.

Endnotes

1. Clyde L. Manschreck, *A History of Christianity in the World* (Englewood Cliffs: Prentice-Hall, 1974), p. 20.

2. Hans Küng, *The Church* (New York: Image Books, 1976), pp. 353-4.

3. Hans Küng, and Walter Kasper, eds., *Polarization in the Church* (New York: Herder and Herder, 1973), p. 7.

4. Roland H. Bainton, *Here I Stand: A Life of Martin Luther* (New York: New American Library, 1950), p. 41.

5. Bainton, p. 45.

6. Curtis I. Crenshaw and Grover E. Gunn, III, *Dispensationalism: Today, Yesterday, and Tomorrow* (Memphis: Footstool Publications, 1989), preface.

7. Bruce Barron's book *The Health and Wealth Gospel* (InterVarsity Press, 1987), offers an excellent assessment of these teachings.

8. Vincent Taylor, *The Names of Jesus* (London: MacMillan & Co. Ltd, 1962), p. 148.

9. "A Cry in the Wilderness," *San Jose Mercury News*, May 10, 1986, Sec. D, p. 13D.

10. Dietrich Bonhoeffer, *The Cost of Discipleship* (New York: The MacMillan Co., 1963), p. 269.

11. J. Gresham Machen, *The Virgin Birth of Christ* (Grand Rapids: Baker Book House, 1930), pp. 2-7.

12. Joseph A. Fitzmyer, S.J., *Luke the Theologian: Aspects of His Teaching* (New York/Mahwah: Paulist Press, 1989), pp. 35-37.

13. Thomas Bokenkotter, *Essential Catholicism* (Garden City: Image Books, 1986), pp. 64-65.

14. Bainton, p. 54.

15. Warren W. Wiersbe, *The Integrity Crisis* (Nashville: Oliver Nelson, 1988), p. 52.

16. Küng, p. 492.

17. Manschreck, p. 86.

18. Küng and Kaspar, p. 85.

19. Richard John Neuhaus, "Religion and Politics Separate but Equal," *San Jose Mercury News*, Sec. C, April 12, 1986, p. 12C.

20. David Jacobsen, *Hostage* (New York: Donald I. Fine, Inc., 1991), p. 79.

21. Demetrius J. Constantelos, *Understanding the Greek Orthodox Church* (New York: Seabury Press, 1982), pp. 96 and 98.

Index

Augustine, 28, 145-146

Bainton, Roland H., 44, 117
Bokenkotter, Thomas, 96
Bonhoeffer, Dietrich, 73
Bultmann, Rudolf, 49

Calvin, John, 147
Calvinism, 30, 34
Chalcedon, Council of, 61-62
Christian reconstructionism, 34
Church:
    establishment of, 17-20
    false church, 5-7
    joy of early church, 21, 61, 63, 67, 152, 167-168
    love of, 3-4, 7-8, 13, 17, 22-23, 27-28, 35-36, 126-129, 148-150, 179
    persecution of, 3-4, 20-21, 25-28, 91, 175
    (and) politics, 20, 169-174
    a spiritual kingdom, 23, 114, 161, 173
Colson, Charles, 14
Constantelos, Demetrios J., 180

Didache, The, 24
dispensationalism, 45
Dulles, Avery, 14
du Plessis, David, 138-139

Eucharist, 15
Evangelicals and Catholics Together: The Christian Mission in the Third Millennium, 5, 14

Fitzmyer, Joseph A., 87
Francis of Assisi, 29
fundamentalism, 6, 33-34, 45-48, 88, 114, 122, 138-140, 170-172

Graham, Billy, 144

Ignatius, 24-27, 86
Irenaeus, 26

Jesus Christ:
    authority of , 17-18
    founder of the Church, 20, 28, 72-74, 174, 182-183
    healing ministry, 19, 62, 161
    love and forgiveness, 17-20, 22, 44, 58, 66-67, 71, 174
    power in salvation, 3, 54, 57-58, 72, 92, 97, 100, 131, 160-161
    sacrificial death, 69-70
    Son of God, 6, 20, 59-60, 65-66, 70-74, 83-84, 87-88, 93, 153
    virgin birth of, 84-88
Jesus Seminar, 49-50

Küng, Hans, 32-33, 128, 154

liberalism, 6, 11, 33, 49-52, 88, 114, 122, 143, 170-172, 183

liberation theology, 34, 171-172
Lustiger, Cardinal Jean-Marie, 72
Luther, Martin, 6-7, 30, 43-44, 47-48, 105, 117-119

MacArthur, John, Jr., 14-15

Manschreck, Clyde L., 31, 146
Middle East hostages, 178

Neuhaus, Richard John, 171

Polycarp, 29
Pope Francis, 131
Pope John XXIII, 16
Pope John Paul II, 15-16, 32, 37, 97
prosperity gospel, 46, 123

Schweitzer, Albert, 49
Second Vatican Council, 16, 181
sexual abuse in the Church, 1-3, 53, 100, 106, 182
Shepherd of Hermas, The, 24
submission teaching, 40-45

Taylor, Vincent, 59

Ut Unum Sint, 16, 37

von Staupitz, Johann, 43-47

Wesley, John, 30

*F*rom the same author...
*N*ew *R*elease

AVAILABLE FROM AMAZON.COM
ISBN: 978-0-9724869-7-2
TRADE PAPER   173 P   PUB 2018 $9.99
KINDLE EBOOK $4.99

The Power of Christ in YOUR Life

The power of Christ is reality and transformation, life-changing power to conquer any sinful habit or addiction. It is power to see miracles and healing in the lives of those prayed for through the Holy Spirit. Warren R. Angel tells story after story of amazing miracles and healing throughout the history of the Church, beginning with the life of Christ and continuing with the apostles—people like Constantine, Augustine, and Luther, and down to our time everywhere in the world where Christ is preached and believed, including his own ministry. Anyone can have his power in their life!

How do you feel about God's love for you?

God's Love in the End Times

Do you think that God could ever stop loving you? If you think "yes" is the answer, you don't understand God's nature as well as you should. Angel blows away all the false ideas about God's love and tells us what the Scriptures really teach us.
Knowing the truth about God's love for you — personally — will help you and God have a better relationship and enable you to trust God in the end times.

Made in the USA
Monee, IL
07 July 2026